Praise for
STAND IN THE HEAT

"The true test of strength and character is how you react in a crisis – and this book gives you the tools to remain calm, positive and in control 'no matter what happens."

Brian Tracy
Author, *Crunch Point*

"The United States of America was forged by the spirit that is exemplified by these great entrepreneurs. It's time that we *Stand in the HEAT* as a nation and once again find our strength. The lessons shared in Glenn's book will give you resolve and show you the way!"

Ben Gay III
Author, The Closers

"Regardless of industry, the willingness and ability to embrace adversity and turn it into opportunity is paramount to success. The great entrepreneurs in this book stayed cool under pressure long enough to see their dreams become reality - so can you!"

Richard Robbins, CEO
Richard Robbins International

"It requires a ton of positive energy to incubate an idea from inception and build a successful, viable business. Those who have succeeded have done so because they were optimistic, resilient and courageous. I encourage you to read this book and learn from the trials, tribulations and triumphs of the entrepreneurs in this book so you can overcome your own challenges and create your own success story."

Jon Gordon
Best-selling author of *The Energy Bus and Training*
Camp-2

I have always been a believer in the power of reading biographies. Glenn brings you fourteen entrepreneurs whose stories will be an example to you of what is possible if you live with honor, enthusiasm, tenacity and action.

Chip Eichelberger
CSP, International speaker, Author

STAND IN THE HEAT

STAND IN THE HEAT

Lessons from Legendary Entrepreneurs
on Staying Cool under Pressure

Glenn Carver

BOOKLOGIX®
Alpharetta, Georgia

ISBN: 978-1-61005-172-9
Library of Congress Control Number: 2012938522
Printed in the United States of America

∞This paper meets the requirements of ANSI/NISO Z39.48-1992 (Permanence of Paper)

The opinions expressed in this book are those of Glenn Carver and the business professionals interviewed for this book. Opinions are provided for information purposes and are not intended as direct career advice.

No compensation was received by Glenn Carver for any person, product, company, website, or service mentioned in this book. The content of this book is not considered an endorsement of any person, product, company, website, or service.

Cover Design by Mike McDowell, Fifty-Eight Advertising

Dedication

To my miraculous son, Grant, and my beautiful wife, Lisa.

Without you, this book would not be possible.

H.E.A.T.

It is my belief that anything worthwhile in life, particularly in starting a new business, requires that we stand in the HEAT to some degree. HEAT is an acronym for four characteristics that are essential to becoming a successful entrepreneur.

Honor

Enthusiasm

Action

Tenacity

The wonderful people I had the privilege to interview for this book have all exemplified the HEAT characteristics in their personal and professional lives. Throughout this book you will see "HEAT Moments" that highlight situations or opportunities that these great entrepreneurs chose to embrace. I hope you enjoy and learn from their real world experiences!

Table of Contents

Foreword

When I met Glenn Carver through my EpiCenter, home of the Entrepreneurship Hall of Fame, I recognized a man with the same vision and passion for entrepreneurship and free enterprise as myself. When I learned of his dream to write a book, launch a brand, and spend the rest of his professional life carrying the torch of entrepreneurship, I knew we were kindred spirits. So I was honored when he asked me to write the foreword to *Stand in the HEAT: Lessons from Legendary Entrepreneurs on Staying Cool under Pressure.*

I have been a serial entrepreneur and a social entrepreneur for more than thirty-five years. Actually, I've been an entrepreneur since I was five years old and began selling pretzels from a street cart with my grandfather in Queens, New York. After learning many invaluable on-the-street lessons as a young adult, I spent the next three decades identifying voids and needs in the consumer marketplace.

As an accomplished and celebrated photographer, I have a keen eye and a unique ability to see what others may not see. Call it vision or acute awareness, but I can anticipate what is coming and position myself and the people around me to prosper and profit.

Case in point: I became one of the nation's youngest head tennis professionals when I was twenty-one years old. My ability to coach and work with all levels of players and people became one of my strongest skill sets, both on and off the court. Before founding the Mitch Schlimer Tennis Centers in Houston, Texas, I realized that many tennis students had difficulty fully understanding the spin of a tennis ball when it was hit because they couldn't visually see the spin of the ball. Identifying a need, I created the two-tone (orange and yellow) tennis ball, which is still sold in stores today, over thirty years later.

One of my dreams had always been to create the "ESPN of entrepreneurship," and I took massive action on that dream in 1993. I created and launched Let's Talk Business Network and the national *Let's Talk Business Radio*, which are dedicated to entrepreneurship, small business, franchising, and youth empowerment. Through *Let's Talk Business Radio* and Let's Talk Business Live, I have interviewed some of the greatest entrepreneurs of our time, including Sir Richard Branson (Virgin), Ben Cohen and Jerry Greenfield (Ben & Jerry's), Fred DeLuca (Subway), the late Anita Roddick (The Body Shop), and more than 750 other entrepreneurs, CEOs, authors, and business leaders.

Considered by many to be the "voice of entrepreneurship" and an "entrepreneur's entrepreneur," I have had the honor of being featured in *The New York Times, The Wall Street Journal, Newsday, SUCCESS* magazine, CNN, and other media venues over the last thirty years. I have also been voted one of the 100 most important radio talk-show hosts in America by my peers; more than 4,500 radio hosts were in the running.

I share all of this with you not to pat myself on the back but to let you know that I know the "belly of the entrepreneurial beast." I have been there and done it, and I have known and worked with thousands of other entrepreneurs. I also know that the failure rate of start-ups in this country and around the world is unacceptably high. Through the EpiCenter, I have made it my life's mission to turn that dial in the direction of a continued and substantially improved rate of entrepreneurial success. Glenn Carver joins me in that mission.

Stand in the HEAT is one of the ways in which Glenn is helping to advance entrepreneurship in America. In this inspiring and insightful book, Glenn shares the stories and advice of fifteen successful entrepreneurs as well as his own journey as an entrepreneur. In the process, he reveals what it's really like and what it really takes to "make it" as an entrepreneur.

As for my part in facilitating entrepreneurship in America, in addition to founding Let's Talk Business Network and *Let's Talk Business Radio* nearly twenty years ago, I founded the original Entrepreneurship Hall of Fame (www.theehalloffame.com) in 2002. My vision was to build a physical facility to house the Entrepreneurship Hall of Fame (EHOF), similar to existing halls of fame, such as the Pro Football Hall of Fame and the Rock and Roll Hall of Fame. As I worked toward that goal, however, I realized that the world of entrepreneurship needed more than a place to acknowledge and learn about the most successful entrepreneurs in history and our time. In order to vastly improve the success rate of start-ups in the United States and around the globe, the fragmented world of entrepreneurship needed to come together and aggregate its knowledge and resources. And we needed an organization and a place with which to do that.

In late 2011, working from offices in Long Island and Atlanta, I founded the EpiCenter—the center for entrepreneurship, philanthropy, and innovation. EpiCenter is also the home of the Entrepreneurship Hall of Fame, dedicated to "illuminating the past, empowering the present, and inspiring the future" of entrepreneurship around the globe. In 2012, we moved into our new EpiCenter headquarters in downtown Atlanta. Now, we are focused on developing the EpiCenter into the world's preeminent center for entrepreneurship and on building a magnificent facility in which to house it.

Glenn and I, along with a growing legion of entrepreneurs, are dedicated to empowering today's and tomorrow's entrepreneurs around the world and helping them to vastly improve their chances of success.

We invite you to join us on this remarkable journey, mission, and revolution!

Mitch Schlimer
Founder and Executive Director
EpiCenter, home of the Entrepreneurship Hall of Fame

The Entrepreneur's Dance

For many years I have had an intense desire to be a successful entrepreneur. Like many of you, I have had a few great ideas that I thought needed to be brought to the marketplace. How many times in your life have you had a great idea and not taken action on it, only to find out in the years to come that someone else had taken action and was making big bucks with *your* idea? Is that not an empty feeling?

Why is it that we can have a great idea that inspires us to our core and has the potential to make us rich, but we still fail to follow through? Personally, I have always made the excuse that I didn't have the money or "working capital" in the moment to follow through on an idea. What a crock! There is money *everywhere* and great ideas will always attract money like a magnet.

I am convinced that the problem is never money. The real problem is FEAR! What if I go for my dream and fail? Where will I be then? What if I'm not as good as I believe I am? What if I leave the "security" of my job that is paying my mortgage and feeding my family and I fall on my face? Then what?

As I wrote these words, I was living and breathing "the entrepreneur's dance." I struggled with the intense, burning-hot desire to strike out on my own as a full-time speaker and author and leave behind the security of a phenomenal company where I worked. I struggled with the belief that if I were a truly successful entrepreneur, I wouldn't be working for someone else in the first place. I struggled with a black-and-white, all-or-nothing mindset. Either you work for someone else or you are an entrepreneur. There is no in between.

But then I realize that entrepreneurship is not purely a destination or an outcome. Entrepreneurship is a *mindset!* There is no shame in working for someone else and paying your bills while you pursue your dream. As long as you are adding value to your employer and the marketplace while you are employed, you can choose to view that employment as win-win.

Entrepreneurship is about having a grand vision for the future, but being flexible enough in the present moment to do whatever it takes, as long as it takes, to make that vision a reality. For most of us, nobody is going to come along and drop a large sum of money in our lap so that we can leave our job and blaze full-time into our venture.

As you read the stories from the entrepreneurs in this book, keep in mind that nobody came along and dropped a large sum of money in their laps either. They did whatever they had to do over the long haul to make their dream a reality. Entrepreneurs embrace the dance of risk and reward. It is a choice.

Acknowledgements

I would like to start by thanking my beautiful wife, Lisa, who has been supportive of my dreams from the day we met. It has been said that beside every great man walks a great woman. Lisa, you are a great woman and a great mom. I love and appreciate you!

Michael McKeller (www.ExtremeMike.com) and I have been the best of friends for the past twenty-six years. Despite his physical challenges, he has remained positive and grateful through circumstances that would have left most of us crying and sucking our thumbs in a world of self-pity. Michael, you are my personal hero and the ultimate Ambassador of Attitude!

My father, Glenn Carver Sr., and I have been best friends for the past forty-five years. He is the ultimate optimist and he epitomizes the "never give up" attitude. To this day he is reinventing himself and following his passion like he is still in his thirties. Dad, when I think of you I think of the classic line that passed your lips one night in the late eighties on our deck on Hilton Head. With a gleam in your eye and the purest conviction, you eloquently stated, "I have no limits!" Dad, you're my dad – I love you man!

Ahmad Meradji, owner of Booklogix (www.Booklogix.com), and his daughter Angela DeCaires have been a godsend. Thank you both so very much for guiding me through this foreign process of publishing my first book. Ahmad, from the first time we met, you have been a true gentleman and a first class professional. You have great passion for your work and I would strongly recommend you to anyone considering the world of self-publishing.

I would like to give a double dose of thanks to my friend, Mike McDowell (www.FiftyEightAdvertising.com), who created an amazing graphic design for my book cover. The first time I saw his work I was literally blown away. I truly believe people took me seriously from the start because of the credibility of the cover. Mike, you are the man!

Derek Brooks, the owner of Brandywine Printing (BrandywinePrinting.com), is a friend and selfless man who took the time to create a mock book for me. The mock book had the finished cover with empty pages that allowed me to continually "sell the dream" to myself and potential interviewees. I took a picture of the mock book on the best-seller shelf at Barnes & Noble and put the picture on my vision board. Thank you Derek.

My friend, Jon Gordon (www.JonGordon.com), is a best-selling author and keynote speaker who has greatly inspired me over the years. His loving spirit and constant humility never cease to amaze me. I will never forget the time he said to me in true Jon Gordon fashion, "Hey, if I can do it, you can do it!" Jon, I aspire to share the stage with you someday my friend!

Although I have yet to meet them personally, I greatly appreciate and immensely thank Glenn Beck and Lee Iacocca for writing their respective books, *Common Sense* and *Where Have All the Leaders Gone?* These two books have touched me at the core of my being and literally changed my life, inducing a significant, emotional experience that I will never forget. Glenn and Lee, you are great Americans!

Thank you SO much to the fourteen incredible men and women who allowed me to interview them for this book! I am honored and humbled that you accepted my invitation. You epitomize the spirit that has made the United States of America the greatest country in the history of civilization. I would be remiss if I didn't give a special "shout out" to George McKerrow. You were the first person to gracefully grant me an interview and let's face it – you never forget your first. Thank you George!

I would like to especially thank our Founding Fathers and all of the inspired entrepreneurs in this great country who go to work every day with vision, passion, and determination. Your unwavering entrepreneurial spirit is the mother of this nation and the free enterprise system that has granted the rest of us our freedoms. On behalf of all Americans, I would like to say that I am eternally grateful.

Most importantly, I would like to thank God who sent me my miraculous son, Grant. Without him I would never have been "standing in the heat" and you would not be reading these words. I love you both eternally!

Introduction

In August of 2009, my fiancée, Lisa, our unborn son, Grant, and I were en route to upstate New York from Atlanta to visit her family. We were enjoying a layover in Chicago at O'Hare Airport and I was passing the time by reading the book *Glenn Beck's Common Sense – The Case Against an Out-of-Control Government, Inspired by Thomas Paine. Common Sense* is Beck's modern interpretation of the original version written by Thomas Paine, which helped spark the American Revolution.

Beck makes a passionate case for us to speak out about the direction in which our great country is headed. He states, "The time has come for a second American Revolution – bring your passion, but leave your muskets at home. This revolution will take place in our minds and hearts." He continues with a call to action that I will never forget. "DO NOT WAIT FOR OTHERS TO DO AND SAY THE THINGS YOU FEEL. The American Republic will not be swept away into the dustbin of history if good men come forward now. Rest assured that others more timid than you will join in the fight, but they wait for you."

Upon reading that passage, I slipped into a deep state of contemplation and reflected upon these pivotal times in which we live. I never served my country in the armed forces, but I felt a calling in that moment to serve my country by joining the fight with my voice and with my passion! I looked at my pregnant fiancée with our unborn son in her belly and I became overwhelmed with responsibility and emotion. My eyes did not merely tear—sitting in a crowded Chicago O'Hare airport with nowhere to hide, I began to sob. As I wiped the wave of streaming tears from my face, I knew in that moment that I had to find my voice and take a stand for entrepreneurship, our country, and our Founding Fathers who made all of this possible.

Fast forward to the morning of February 2, 2010 where I was stuck in rush hour traffic on I-75 South in Atlanta. At the time, I was forty-two years old with a fiancée and a beautiful, three month old, firstborn son at home. As you can imagine, I was completely motivated and inspired to provide for this new miracle that had recently entered my life. Prior to his birth, I had been a selfish bachelor living for the day. On November 21, 2009, everything changed.

Becoming a father has been the best thing that has ever happened to me times a thousand. The responsibility and unconditional love for my son has completely changed me and shifted my focus. God knows what is in our best interest and I needed to be held accountable and responsible! I have always struggled with commitment in my personal and business life and it has certainly shown in my results.

I am a public speaker by trade and the 2009 holiday season left me with an extremely light speaking schedule in the first quarter of 2010. I was actually very grateful for the extra time I had during that period and I took advantage of the situation by spending every moment with Lisa and Grant. However, with a bank account that was on vapors, I was scared, anxious, and under a significant level of stress.

On that brisk February morning in the solitude of my car, I heard an exceptionally clear voice (my subconscious, God, or someone in between) say "Glenn, stand in the heat – don't freak out." In that instant, I realized that I was not alone. I surmised that there are probably more people "standing in the heat" financially today than at any other point in our lifetime. Perhaps more people are "standing in the heat" today than since the Great Depression?

Entrepreneurship is the choice to see the opportunity in every adversity and the ability to bring problem solving solutions to the market place. However, entrepreneurship can be mean, tough, and nasty. At times it can feel very lonely and discouraging. I believe the entrepreneurial spirit of our Founding Fathers is as important and vital today as it was when they envisioned and created the revolution that we call the United States of America. Do you have the entrepreneurial spirit?

Meet the Entrepreneurs

When I first envisioned this book, I knew I needed to include entrepreneurs from a variety of backgrounds and industries. My search led me to the fine folks who will share their stories with you in the pages ahead.

While there are many differences in their stories, they all have a couple of things in common: fierce determination; confidence in their decisions; and success in the path of their choosing. I was honored to speak with them in-depth about their past, present, and future.

Mo Anderson
Vice Chairman, Keller Williams Realty

Mo Anderson's first love was piano. She taught music for fourteen years before she entered the real estate field. Mo says her husband was the one who suggested she make a career change and leave teaching. She opened a Century 21 franchise office in 1975. In 1986, she sold that company to Merrill Lynch Realty, where she held the position of district vice president until December 1989.

Now in her role as Vice Chairman of Keller Williams Realty, Mo puts her teaching skills to use, traveling to various cities and teaching at Keller Williams's training events. She was named one of America's Top 25 Influential Thought Leaders by REALTOR magazine in December of 2006.

Joyce Bone
CEO and Founder, JBE
Founder of MillionaireMoms.com

Joyce Bone cofounded EarthCare, an environmental company, which grew in just eighteen months from zero to $50 million. She took the company public and reached $125 million in annual revenues. Once Joyce left her company she started the real estate investment firm Emerald Real Estate, LLC. Joyce is a columnist for *Glow* magazine and hosts the *Inside the Winner's Circle* radio show. Her story of going from a stay-at-home mom to a successful CEO today inspires women everywhere. Joyce encourages other entrepreneurs, especially moms, to reach for their dreams.

Herman Cain
Founder of T.H.E New Voice, Inc.
Former 2012 Presidential Candidate

You may recognize Herman Cain most for his candidacy for the 2012 Republican Party presidential nomination. He is a syndicated columnist and also does radio commentary. Cain has held positions as a systems analyst at Coca-Cola, vice president at Pillsbury, and regional vice president for Burger King. The entrepreneur in Cain really came out in 1986, when he accepted the role of president and CEO of Godfather's Pizza, a struggling chain. Cain turned things around at Godfather's in a little over a year, reducing the number of stores and boosting sales at the stores he kept open. He and some other executives later purchased the chain from Pillsbury. Cain was later named head of the National Restaurant Association.

Bob Doyle
Founder, Wealth Beyond Reason

Bob Doyle is one of the stars and teachers of the international phenomenon, The Secret. He is also the best-selling author of *Follow Your Passion - Find Your Power*, and the creator and facilitator of the Wealth Beyond Reason law of attraction curriculum.

In 2002, Bob decided to quit his corporate job and leave the security of getting a regular paycheck. In a search for answers, he found himself studying principles of living life by design, and poured himself into the science of this idea. A simple education in the quantum physics of thought led Bob to the breakthroughs he needed to turn his financial situation around, and share his value with the world in a big way.

Since that time, Bob has been educating thousands about the science of the law of attraction, and how to utilize that education to create inspiring visions filled with passion, purpose, and abundance. He has spoken all over the world, and reaches millions through his online programs. In addition to his work with the law of attraction, Bob is also an avid ukulele player, composes music, does voiceover work, writes, and is involved in many facets of computer imaging and animation.

Scott Goodknight
Founder, Break Your Fear Adventure Club and Peak Performance Trainer

Scott Goodknight is fearless. As the founder of the Break Your Fear Adventure Club, the former U.S. Army Ranger, also known as "The Breakthru Guy," helps people overcome their fears. Scott has a simple philosophy: "Anyone can do anything; fear is the only thing that stops you." His mission is to help people "break thru" their fears so they can live the life of their dreams.

With zero knowledge or experience in the field of publishing, Scott wrote, published, sold, and distributed over 50 thousand books and 2.5 million travel maps for motorcyclists in just over four years. In 2006, Scott entered the arena of Personal and Professional Development to help people break free of the excuses, negative beliefs, and fear that stop them from being successful in their personal lives and businesses. Scott is the author of *A Courageous Mind*, and is currently the producer of the "Break Your Fear" documentary series.

Dr. Kathleen Hall
Founder and CEO, The Stress Institute & The Mindful Living Network

Dr. Kathleen Hall is an internationally recognized expert in stress and work-life balance. As the founder and CEO of The Stress Institute and The Mindful Living Network, media seek Dr. Hall's knowledge and expertise in times of tragedy or crisis, such as the West Virginia and Utah coal miner tragedies, the aftermath of hurricane Katrina, the London terrorist bombing, and more.

Dr. Hall has written three books, has been interviewed by major national television media, and appeared in hundreds of articles in magazines and newspapers across the country. Her diverse background includes degrees in Finance, Divinity, and Spirituality. She has a passion for animals, rescuing and fostering animals at her farm, where she also runs a bird sanctuary.

Pano Karatassos
Founder and President, Buckhead Life
Restaurant Group

Award-winning chef and restaurateur Pano Karatassos grew up in the restaurant industry. His father owned a restaurant import food business, and once in the Navy Pano worked in the food department. After his service, Pano studied at the Culinary Institute of America and then began working in kitchens all over the country. In 1979, Pano opened his first restaurant, Pano's & Paul's.

Today, Pano has more than a dozen dining establishments, and is the founder and president of the Buckhead Life Restaurant Group where he develops the concept of each of his independent restaurants and oversees the day-to-day operations of his restaurants as well as regulating food, personnel, and decor quality standards.

Lisa Levison
CEO, derma-glove, Inc.
Owner, Decontamination Restoration Services

Lisa Levison is the Founder of derma-glove and the owner of Decontamination Restoration Services (DRS). In 1989, Lisa founded Innovative Design Ideas, an office furniture retailer. She learned from her clients that there wasn't much available in the way of servicing existing furniture, so she refocused her business to offer services for all office furniture needs. The company then expanded to include a division called Decontamination Restoration Service, DRS, which offers specialty cleaning, such as mold remediation, crime scene cleanup, and disaster recovery.

Lisa and DRS began to see a need for something to protect those who encounter contaminated environments from hand-acquired infectious diseases, and derma-glove was born. derma-glove is a moisturizing, sanitizing hand protectant that adheres to the skin's outer layers.

Dave Liniger
Co-Founder and Chairman of the Board, RE/MAX, LLC

Dave Liniger became interested in real estate after buying and selling property while stationed in Arizona with the US Air Force. He and his wife Gail co-founded RE/MAX in Denver, Colorado in 1973.

They started the company after being dissatisfied with the way the real estate business was operating at the time.

Liniger is recognized as an expert in recruiting and motivation, sales training and time management. He has been inducted into the Council of Real Estate Brokerage Managers (CRB) Hall of Leaders and the Real Estate Buyer's Agent Council (ABR) Hall of Fame. He has been featured in *Forbes*, *Bloomberg BusinessWeek*, and *Entrepreneur* magazines, and inducted into the International Franchise Hall of Fame. He co-founded of the Denver-area conservation Center, The Wildlife Experience, and also owns the Sanctuary Golf Course.

Trish McCarty
President & CEO, StarShine Planet
Founder/President, StarShine Academy
Schools, StarShine Academy
International Schools/Education
Resources, LLC, StarShine Charter
Schools

Trish McCarty has been called "Mother Teresa with an MBA." She spent two decades as a financial professional, whose incorporation of technology in the banking industry brought her national attention. After feeling frustrated while looking for suitable and safe learning establishments for her children, Trish acted on her belief that every person deserves to be educated with the best resources available. So in 2000 she formed Education Resources, to address critical problems in the education market.

In 2002, she opened a K-12 school for high-risk, inner-city Phoenix children, and named it the StarShine Academy. Her goal was to prove that with the right help, all children will learn to reach for the stars. Trish has authored books and hundreds of newspaper and magazine articles. She has been featured in *Inc. Magazine, The New York Times, Working Woman,* and more. She has received a number of awards, including the Working Woman's Entrepreneurial Excellence Award, and was named one of the Top 100 Women of Arizona in 2000.

George McKerrow
Founder, LongHorn Steakhouse
Co-Founder, Ted's Montana Grill

George McKerrow Jr. has the distinction of being the first entrepreneur interviewed for *Stand in the HEAT.*

He is a forty-year veteran of the restaurant business, having started out as a teenager. He opened the first LongHorn Steakhouse in 1981 and evolved that one location in Atlanta into RARE Hospitality International, which was sold to Darden Restaurants in 2007. In 1996 he co-founded We're Cookin' Inc., then went on to serve on the board of directions for the National Restaurant Association and the Culinary Institute of Atlanta.

In 2002, George co-founded Ted's Montana Grill with partner Ted Turner. George serves as CEO of the restaurant company, which is based in Atlanta, and has almost fifty locations in sixteen states. He was awarded the first Lifetime Achievement Award from the Georgia Restaurant Association in 2007.

Wendy Reed
Executive Vice President Strategic Alliances, The TAS Group

Wendy Reed began her career in information technology with Accenture, and went on to hold sales, marketing, and sales management positions with organizations such as MSA (which later became Dun & Bradstreet Software), Viasoft, and Clarus. Wendy is the former founder and CEO of InfoMentis, which was later acquired by The TAS Group.

Wendy is an author and the recipient of awards and recognition from organizations including the American Business Women's Association, *Inc. Magazine*, Ernst & Young, WIT (Women In Technology), and *Catalyst* magazine.

Mitch Schlimer
Founder and Executive Director, EpiCenter, home of the Entrepreneurship Hall of Fame

Mitch Schlimer has been a serial and social entrepreneur for more than thirty-five years. In addition to being an inventor and accomplished photographer, Mitch has founded six businesses, including Mitch Schlimer Tennis Centers, a video production business, and an advertising agency called Impac International. He is also a co-founder and board member of the Magic Wand Foundation, an amazing organization dedicated to empowering youth around the world and sharing "the 7 mindsets to live your ultimate life."

In 1993, with a vision to create the "ESPN for entrepreneurs," Mitch founded Let's Talk Business Network (LTBN), which provides consulting, coaching, educational, and other support services to entrepreneurs, business owners, CEOs, and youth. As the creator and host of the national *Let's Talk Business Radio*, Mitch has interviewed more than 750 (and counting) successful entrepreneurs and authors, including such notables as Sir Richard Branson, Wally Amos, Anita Roddick, Fred DeLuca, Jim Collins, and Jack Canfield.

Mitch's passion for the advancement and expansion of entrepreneurship around the globe led him to found the original Entrepreneurship Hall of Fame (EHOF) in 2002. Then, in late 2011, he founded the EpiCenter—the global center for entrepreneurship, philanthropy, and innovation as well as the home of EHOF. Mitch serves as Executive Director of both the EpiCenter and the Entrepreneurship Hall of Fame.

Brad Sugars
Founder, ActionCOACH

Brad Sugars started his first business at age fifteen, employing his friends as newspaper delivery boys and taking a piece of the profits. By the time he was twenty-one, he was running four retail stores and a photocopy management contract. He says his mother almost had a heart attack when he told her that he wanted to quit and go into work for himself.

In 1993 Brad started the ActionCOACH brand (formerly known as Action International) when he was in his early twenties. He built the business coaching firm company from nothing to more than a thousand franchisees in twenty-seven countries. Sugars has bought and sold fifty-seven businesses and authored fourteen books.

Heather Thomson
Yummie by Heather Thomson

Before founding Yummie, Heather Thomson had spent fifteen years as a successful designer and stylist. She had worked with some of entertainment's biggest stars. She was the founding Design Director for Sean "Diddy" Combs's line, and worked alongside Beyonce Knowles and Jennifer Lopez to create and launch their respective lines.

Yummie was "born" shortly after Heather's children. She was disappointed by women's shapewear and created her own patented three-section system, which is now Yummie Tummie's signature. Yummie Tummie was featured on the Oprah Winfrey show as one of Oprah's Favorite Things, and the brand is a favorite of celebrities including Beyonce, Tyra Banks, and Carrie Underwood.

Section I

Manage Your Emotions

"It's the whole kindergarten thing, Mom. I'm alone in there, swimming with the sharks."

I suppose most people in the world have a gap between where they are and where they truly want to be. I believe *all* entrepreneurs have that gap, otherwise they would not have embarked on their venture in the first place. The gap can be emotional, spiritual, financial, or any combination thereof.

I also suppose that many entrepreneurial ventures are born out of a catharsis. My vision for this book was born out of the financial pressure and awesome responsibility of having a newborn at home, combined with an empty bank account. On that February morning when I very clearly heard, "Glenn, stand in the heat, don't freak out," I knew the first step in closing my own gap was managing my emotions. Specifically, I knew that I had to release my fear.

Fear serves a purpose and its message is preparation. However, most of us fear events that never come to fruition. Whether in business, sports, politics, or in battle, the person who can maintain their composure and stay cool under pressure the longest will eventually prevail. Consequently, I took full responsibility for the condition of my life and didn't point my finger anywhere else. I realized that my financial condition was a product of my choices and I was the only one to blame. Accepting full responsibility for the condition of your life is a liberating experience and it creates the space for growth.

My personal technique for managing my emotions and releasing fear is twofold. First, I say to myself, "It's only money. There is an endless supply of money flowing through the system and all I have to do is tap into it." Second, I remind myself that there is no stress in the world. Stress resides solely in the mind of man. Think about it. If I were to snap my fingers and humanity were instantly erased from the planet, would there be any stress? If I gave you $1 million to walk outside and point to the stress, could you do it?

Finally, I am learning how to put my ego in my back pocket in a constant pursuit of humility. One of my mentors, Dr. Wayne Dyer, says ego stands for "Edging God Out." He also says, "Let go and let God." This philosophy truly resonates with me and reminds me that we already have everything we need within us. Nearly everything we fear and stress over is created through our own limited thinking. Let's face it; if you have a roof over your head and your basic bills are paid, everything else is gravy!

STAND IN THE HEAT
Chapter One

Are You Crazy?

"All truth passes through three stages. First, it is ridiculed. Second, it is violently opposed. Third, it is accepted as being self-evident."

- Arthur Schopenhauer
German Philosopher

If you are truly an entrepreneur with fresh, innovative, cutting edge ideas, be prepared to be called crazy. Be prepared to be called crazy by some of the people closest to you. As a matter of fact, most great inventors, entrepreneurs, and creators of social change know that they have a great idea even when they are being laughed at and ridiculed. Remember, there is no such thing as bad publicity. Madonna once said that she didn't care if people were saying good or bad things about her as long as they were talking.

I have always been a fan of thinking very big. I don't know if I adopted that philosophy from my father, the many great books I have read, or both. I do know that thinking can be the hardest work in which humans can engage. I once told my little league football coach, Coach Sharbaugh, "If you have to hit, you might as well hit hard." Consequently, if you have to think, you might as well think BIG.

Since college, I have subscribed to *Success* magazine which is an absolutely indispensable resource for entrepreneurs. Every month the publisher, Darren Hardy, interviews great thinkers about their philosophy and strategies for success and he puts the interviews on a CD which is included in the magazine. In a 2011 issue, Darren Hardy interviewed Mel Robbins, who is a former criminal defense attorney, columnist for *Success* magazine, radio host, author, and nationally acclaimed life coach. In her interview, she suggests that we should have some major goals in life that are "embarrassing." We should have at least one goal that is so BIG that we would be embarrassed to tell our friends at a dinner party. I love it! I can assure you that if some of my friends saw the goals and affirmations posted on my bathroom mirror, they would say, "Glenn, you are *crazy*!"

Hot Thought

*Have a goal so BIG that
it's embarrassing.*

Sound business and investing advice tells us to discover what the competition is doing and do the opposite. Find out where the "herd" is going and move in the opposite direction. I have always enjoyed the contrarian point of view. I believe entrepreneurs are contrarians due to the fact that they want to chart their own course and leave their mark on the world in some way. In my opinion, thinking big and thinking differently are a virtue. However, be prepared to be ridiculed and violently opposed in the beginning. Be prepared to be called *Crazy*!

Value Your Opinion of Yourself
More than the Opinions of Others

Others may call you crazy, even family and friends, but it's how you feel about yourself and your endeavor that matters most. One-time presidential hopeful Herman Cain had to ignore the people closest to him who thought he was crazy. He'd remind them, "Thank you very much for that input, but this is my dream, not yours!"

Herman says his wife has called him crazy in a good way, and still does. When he said he wanted to go back into the corporate world for a job in Atlanta, his wife supported the move because their families were there. But then, Herman says, came the real test. "I went to her and said, 'I want to take a new job up in Minnesota,' and we're going to leave Atlanta where her folks were and my folks were and we were raising our first child there. See, she was also willing to share in me pursuing my professional dream."

Pioneers Usually Get the Arrows in the Back

When Mo Anderson was fulfilling her vision of the Keller Williams model, she says some people didn't believe in what she was doing. "They said it would never work, and that I was an idiot to do it, and of course, that's what happens to you when you are a pioneer. You have to be prepared to pull the arrows out of your back. You have to be prepared to ford the rivers and cross the streams and just keep on going."

In the beginning, Mo was laughed at and ridiculed. Not anymore! "When people would see my name badge and it would say Keller Williams Realty some of them would literally turn and walk away. Because they didn't want to spend any time with anybody so ridiculous to be implementing this new model that wouldn't work." But now, Mo says, "I go to the big boy meetings and they can't wait to talk to me."

The poetic justice, Mo tells me, is that in terms of size, Keller Williams is the number two Real Estate organization in the United States. "It doesn't get any better than that. We're on our way to number one. And they said it wouldn't work."

Believe in Your Success in Every Molecule of Your Being

Early on in her career, Joyce Bone gave herself a very narrow window of time and a big goal to accomplish. When she was twenty-eight, Joyce decided that she wanted to be a millionaire by the time she was thirty! She said most people laughed at her. But what made the difference for her? "I truly intended with every molecule of my being to make it a reality. It wasn't a 'maybe' or wishful thinking," she says. She started writing down ideas, three a day for ten days. When she looked back at her list of thirty ideas, she said to herself, "You know, these really kind of stink; this is not going to get me to a million dollars by the time I'm thirty."

But it wasn't about those specific ideas; it was bigger than that. Think of it this way: you get a new car, a Volvo, and suddenly everywhere you look you notice Volvos. "It was the same concept when I was trying to come up with an idea for the business that was going to make me a millionaire," said Joyce. "I just had it on my mind all the time. I was keeping my ears open." When she still hadn't come to that "big idea," she decided to have lunch with an old boss. She told him she was trying to come up with an idea for a business. Then, she says, "It hit me like a brick wall. He's sitting right in front of me!" Joyce had watched him build a business then sell it for millions of dollars. She pitched the idea of them starting a business together, buying and consolidating businesses. And EarthCare was born. Joyce attributes her success to keeping her eyes and ears open, and to asking for what you want. "Nothing happens for people who don't open their mouth," she says.

Hot Thought

> *Nothing happens for people who don't open their mouth.*

It Doesn't *Have* to be Hard in the Beginning

"I received unbelievable encouragement from the start," says Heather Thompson, creator of Yummie Tummie shapewear. "I was working for the most beautiful, sought-after talent of the time, Beyonce Knowles. I was working with her mom and her family and I was in love with them. I wasn't thinking of leaving. I wasn't thinking of starting my own business."

Heather didn't realize she was an entrepreneur until she experienced a very personal need. After her first child was born, a large dose of adversity unleashed her entrepreneurial spirit. The essence of entrepreneurship is the ability to convert adversity into opportunity and capitalize on a new idea. "For the first time in my life I was really hit with a weight loss quandary at a time when I was focused only on my child. I went to the shapewear section of the department store to boost my confidence and make me feel better and encourage myself and instead when I got there I was like, whoa, this place is frozen in time."

Heather recognized an opportunity in the shapewear market, so she took massive action. "I'm from the fashion industry. I've been a fashion designer for almost twenty years. All of the products I tried on would bite, they ride, they would roll, they were hot, they were uncomfortable. Then I had what I call a 'Donny Deutsch moment.' There's gotta be a better way!"

Brad Sugars was one of the pioneers of the business coaching industry at a very young age. Coaching has been an integral part of sports for a hundred years, but not everyone understood the importance of having a business coach when Brad started ActionCOACH. He said, "No, I don't think people thought I was crazy. I think people said, 'You gotta remember that youth can be either a negative or a positive.' I always use it as a positive. Once people learned the strategies that I teach they clearly understood that this is actually stuff that works."

It is possible that you will be understood and supported at the beginning of your venture, but don't expect it. In most cases, new ideas are met with skepticism and doubt.

HEAT Moment

Brad Sugars showed tremendous Enthusiasm when he founded ActionCOACH in his twenties.

Humility Facilitates Authentic Power

Regardless of how far you go in achieving your goals, you've got to stay humble. It doesn't matter who you are or what you do. Humility will empower you. For Dr. Kathleen Hall, a discussion with an enormously wealthy woman who needed some counseling, and talk about humility, led to the creation of The Mindful Living Network. The woman had paid for a private session with a high-profile, motivational life coach. She told the coach that even with her company and her healthy finances, she was still miserable, and didn't know what to do about it. After hearing her story, the gentleman said to her, "My suggestion is that you go to the nearest McDonald's and ask for an employment application." He told her to fill out that application and get a job. The woman thought he meant to buy the franchise. "Oh absolutely not," he said, "I want you to work at the front waiting on customers or maybe scrubbing the floor." He wanted her to work her way up. Suffice it to say the woman was very upset.

The woman went home crying, and later started feeling more upset because she couldn't see herself working at McDonald's. She arranged to meet with Dr. Hall, and after hearing her story, Dr. Hall asked the woman why she was reacting this way, and why she had asked to see her. The woman said to her, "The reason I'm sitting here is because I know you'd work at McDonald's."

"And I would have," says Dr. Hall. "I would have gone straight to McDonald's." Dr. Hall says she told the woman, "Your biggest fear is to be common."

Hot Thought

> *Many people simply*
> *fear being common.*

She then told the woman that she had always had an idea that McDonald's would be a great place to start a self-care program.

The woman responded by laughing, but Dr. Hall was very serious about the idea. "I'd go into McDonald's and I would think, I'm gonna get my cardiac rehab group and they can meet at seven in the morning. The cancer groups—a lot of women that have breast cancer—they can meet at like one o'clock after they've driven carpool or gotten their kids. Then at seven at night I would have support groups meet here. We could do our self-care program. It would be awesome.

"Then I'd grow and I'd finally be the manager of the McDonald's...the cleanest, most exciting, vibrant, McDonald's on the planet. I would be on the front of *Forbes* and *Fortune* because of our McDonald's."

She conceived the concept of The Mindful Living Network. Two months later, she was asked to do a speech for McDonald's; she spoke about work-life balance. By staying humble, and being willing to start at the very bottom and work her way up, Dr. Hall took her goals to the next level.

Take Pride in Being a Little Crazy

Many, if not all, entrepreneurs have been told that their ideas won't work, don't make sense, or are "a little crazy" at one time or another. And why not embrace that, suggests Scott Goodknight, who helps people conquer their fears to help them live their dreams. "I take great pride in being called crazy! Don King, was he crazy? Was Evel Knievel crazy? Is Donald Trump crazy? Crazy is good. We had a saying in the Rangers: 'If you're not living on the edge you're taking up too much room.'"

If you're not taking chances, not thinking (or maybe even acting) a bit crazy, are you really giving all you've got to make your dreams a reality? Be proud of those goals, no matter what others might say, because ultimately, yours is the only opinion that will make or break you on the path to achieving success.

Hot Thought

If people are calling you crazy, you might be onto something.

Hot Seat

✓ List two reasons why friends or family might say you're "crazy." Then list two ways you can prove them wrong.

✓ Pick an entrepreneur, history-maker, or leader that might have been considered "crazy" in their time. This will be your "crazy icon." Let's say you choose Steve Jobs. The next time someone pokes fun at your dream, ask them if they think Steve Jobs was crazy when he founded Apple. That will get them thinking!

✓ Think about your goals. List three skills you might not possess that will be needed to run your business or launch your product. How might you get assistance in those areas?

✓ If you start your own business, you may have to "start over" or start at the bottom and work your way up. Write down one way that being humble will help make that path easier.

STAND IN THE HEAT
Chapter Two

Fear

"Every man, through fear, mugs his aspirations a dozen times a day."

- Brendan Francis
Irish poet

If I have succeeded at anything in life, it has been my willingness to face my fears and expand my comfort zone. In life we are either growing or dying. If we are comfortable, we are most likely dying. Most people die in their twenties, but don't get buried until their eighties. I believe most of us don't have what we want in our lives for two reasons: lack of clarity and fear. Lack of clarity and fear are the killers of passion, potential, and purpose.

I remember the first time I spoke in public I was so scared that I almost passed out! I was a senior at the University of Georgia and I was in a management class in which we had to write a business plan. My group of three students wrote a business plan for a small printing business much like Kinko's. Each of us had to present our portion of the business plan to the class and explain how our business would be a success.

Our business plan was very tight, but I was completely unprepared to present my segment on the big day. There were only twenty or so students in my class, but it seemed like a stadium when I took the podium. I'll have to admit that the idea for writing a business plan for a print shop was not my idea and I was somewhat along for the ride. Although I did my fair share of the work, I was never totally interested or engaged. As a result, my passion, or lack thereof, in front of my fellow students must have been evident.

I remember being light-headed and everything seemed blurry. My knees were weak and I was very concerned that I was going to forget my entire presentation. I wanted to vomit! It was at that moment that I realized that I could NOT go through life with that fear. The fear of public speaking is most people's number one fear, but influential and powerful communication is essential for success in business.

Hot Thought

Confront your ultimate fear head on.

Fortunately, we were graded on the merit of our business plan and not the presentation. My team got an A and the experience was the catalyst for overcoming the greatest fear in my life. Shortly after leaving college, I joined a network marketing company in which I really believed. I saw the opportunity to make a lot of money and just as importantly, I saw the opportunity to give group presentations and break through my fear of public speaking.

As it turned out, I did not make a lot of money. However, I did break through my fear. Not only did I break through my fear, I actually got used to speaking in public. Not only did I get used to it, I started to like it. Not only did I start to like it, I began to love it. Not only have I come to love it, it's what I want to do with the rest of my life.

The moral of this story – you never know what lies on the opposite side of your greatest fear. It just might be your life's purpose!

Fear of Failure

If you're like me, your biggest fear, in anything you do, is failure. We're not alone. Heather Thompson, who left a career as a stylist to the stars to start her own shapewear line, says, "Not succeeding is still my biggest fear." It's been less than ten years since she launched her brand, and says the hard part isn't coming up with the idea, but instead maintaining the idea. "My goal for this business, for this brand that I'm building, Yummie by Heather Thomson, is for it to be around a lot longer than me. So, I'm afraid that I won't succeed. That's my biggest fear."

Don't go into a new venture with a negative attitude. Stay focused on your long-term goals for your business, and keep those goals in mind in difficult or unsure times.

Going Broke

Starting any new business is going to require capital and careful financial planning. Whether you've found an investor or you're cashing in that 401(k) to start a new business, be prepared to feel financially unstable, at least in the beginning.

For some, that fear of losing it all may never pass. "I still fear being broke," says Joyce Bone, founder of EarthCare, an environmental company that grew from zero to $50 million in eighteen months. Joyce says the feeling stems from a fear of going back to her childhood, when her family was poor. "I would like to eventually not really think about that," she says. "Things like the stock market and real estate, all these different things that happen, that always rattle my cages. I try not to let that control me." With careful financial planning you can be better prepared for unexpected additional costs or losses.

Uncertainty

Fear of uncertainty—it may be the single biggest reason why people don't make the leap from working for someone else to starting their own business. Will the venture be successful? Will I be able to maintain my current lifestyle? Will revenue exceed expenses in the first year? All these things are uncertain when starting and operating your own business.

Just ask Herman Cain. He cites uncertainty in today's business environment as something that scares him more than anything he's been afraid of in his life when it comes to business and the future of the United States. "This uncertainty scares me to death because I've never seen it this bad."

Herman thinks back to when he was a mathematician working for the Department of the Navy, in the late 1960s. "The earlier part of your career you're just kind of oblivious to how external factors might impact your career and your business." He says businesses took "their lumps" from the government because it was a fact of life. But now, he says, the "lumps" that are being imposed upon businesses "are so earth-shattering that it's scary." Herman says that creates another element of uncertainty, making it difficult to be confident in what you want to do and how you're going to do it. "They could pass a regulation tomorrow that will change your whole game plan."

Government vs. Small Business Owners

So is the government "out to get" small business owners? Whether they are or not, the actions of our government will have a deep impact on your budding venture. Restaurateur Pano Karatassos fears the government's regulations, taxes, and their lack of ability to work well with small businesses. He believes that the administration doesn't understand business. "The government never had to meet a payroll, read a P&L statement or a balance sheet. They never had to do any of these things but they all know how to run your business better and I'm afraid of them."

George McKerrow, co-founder of LongHorn Steakhouse, fears the overburdening of the small business owner in America. "We can't get a break on amortization or depreciation. These are tax breaks that we need to take the risks." Citing the overstaffing of TSA employees at a small airport in South Dakota as an example, George says, "The government's getting bigger and bigger and bigger. More and more employment is being funded and created by our government and less and less by independent businesses. I worry about that."

You're Not Alone

The term "entrepreneur" may refer to just one person, but you really can't achieve your goals without help from others. Scott Goodknight, who specializes in helping people conquer their fears, says a huge key that people miss in becoming a successful entrepreneur, is that they *don't* have to do it alone. "This is the myth of the self-made man and self-made woman. You are not going to do it alone. Nobody ever does it alone," he says. "You've got to work as a team. Think about it. What's more powerful? One warrior or a tribe of warriors? Or a whole army of warriors? What's more powerful? One computer or the internet?"

"You're going to have to learn how to make a map and you're going to have to learn how to show that map to other people and convince them that's in their best interest to support your interests," Scott says.

Hot Thought

*Enroll people in your
vision to elicit their help.*

Compelling Vision

Is your "Big Idea" enough to keep you motivated? Any number of fears could stop you in your tracks as you try to launch a new business or concept. The best way to combat that fear? "I recommend that you have a very compelling vision," says Bob Doyle. One of the stars of *The Secret*, Bob says if you don't have a compelling vision then you'll listen to those "little voices." He says that the belief systems people have are what really stop them from putting their dreams into action. Bob believes that we may get so attached to our original vision that we can't see the fluent nature of the universe, and how energy flows and changes. "Eventually, the little voice will win. You will get stopped over and over again."

How can you keep those "little voices" at bay? You need to have an idea that inspires you! "You have to have a vision that moves you into action to get you where you want to be. Ultimately, you have an idea of who you want to be and the impact you want to have on the world," he says. It's then up to us to take that idea from the universe and put it into action. "It may only be one or two steps that you needed to take, and now the Universe says, 'Okay, now I'm going to give him what he really needs to get where he really wants to go.'"

Bob compares it to the Law of Attraction. You put the idea or vision out there of who you are and what you want to accomplish and see if the universe helps get you there! "You've gotta be willing to go with the flow. That's how it's most effortless. That's how it's more fun. The only thing that makes it tricky is when you start freaking out!" He warns us that it takes practice to hear your intuition. It's hard to know what it feels like. "There's no intuition class at school. We're just not taught to follow our intuition."

Hot Thought

*In spite of the circumstances,
do NOT freak out!*

Healthy Fear

A little fear isn't always a bad thing. Fear may make you cautious in areas where you should make decisions with extra care. Joyce Bone says a dose of fear helped her to be a very good trend spotter. Joyce says, "Before the whole banking crisis meltdown I went and saw my financial planner the week before and said, 'I'm not feeling good about this.'" Her caution saved her in the real estate market as well. "I was heavily in real estate and then I realized anybody who can fog a mirror was getting a loan and I thought that's just not right. So I sold all of my real estate except for this one property that we wanted to keep and I got out."

Hot Thought

At all times be aware of your surroundings.

She says people that worked with her sometimes thought she was crazy. "With my company, when we went public I had my goal and I sold my shares. I passed my goal of becoming a millionaire and I got it in cash. They were like, 'What are you doing? You're crazy. It's gonna go up.'" She kept a saying in mind, "Pigs get fat and hogs get slaughtered." It's an old southern term that means take your profit, but don't get greedy. "If something happens to this company and I was being greedy and I didn't reach my goal, I would never forgive myself," Joyce says. She accepted that she might be leaving something on the table, but that she could take the money and invest it somewhere else. "I've achieved my goal and I'm happy."

What causes people like Joyce to make the right decisions at the right time? "I think people just get numb or too busy to keep their eyes open. I'm always scanning the horizon; I'm always aware of what's going on around me. I think that, even as an entrepreneur, that's a critical skill to have."

Losing Perspective

Your attitude plays a big role in getting you where you want to be. George McKerrow, whose family came to the United States from Scotland, calls his ancestors "the ultimate entrepreneurs." "They worked for themselves. They lived and died by the success of their crops and the health and well-being of their animals." While small businesses are struggling more and more, McKerrow says, "If we don't maintain an optimistic atmosphere and challenge young people to become entrepreneurs and take risks, we're going to die an ugly death."

Attitude is everything. And once your dream business is up and running, don't forget what it has taken for you to get there. You may go from being the only person on your staff, to having hundreds of people working for you. Lisa Levison, who founded derma-glove, says, "I fear that I might lose sight and get too far ahead of myself." She worries about getting caught up in the "hoopla," saying, "I don't want to forget that I'm just a little service girl that needs to be put there pushing a broom." Lisa makes a good point. Don't ever forget where you came from or how you got there. Even a CEO may have to empty out the trash or clean the bathrooms if the need arises. Remember to stay humble and true to your roots, regardless of how tall your tree grows.

Getting "Bored"

Wendy Reed's fear is getting bored. She says after several years, when procedures are fully developed and set, she starts, somewhat, to lose interest in the operational aspects of business. "It's boredom," she says. "You just get into a rut almost, and so then it's not as exciting. More rules are in place." That can get annoying for someone like Wendy, who says she's "not a good rule follower." How can you combat that boredom? By constantly searching for ways to improve your business, whether it's your products, services, methods, or positioning in the industry. Also keep educating yourself. There's always something new to learn, whether it is in regards to your industry, or developing your leadership skills; this can help you fight back that feeling of boredom that may start to set in once your business is in a more comfortable position.

Making a Big Impact

While many people looking to start their own business are hoping to do so for financial gain, others may be hoping to leave something behind. That is the case for Scott Goodknight, who specializes in helping people to conquer their fears. One of Scott's fears? Not having a big impact in his lifetime. "I fear running out of time to share this information with people that may have been like me who came up in an impoverished environment," he says. He believes that those raised in emotionally impoverished or unsupportive environments don't have the belief system to go after their dreams. "My vision is to create a community of millions of people all over the world who are living, breathing, using these principles in their life for whatever endeavor that they want to and they're supporting each other."

Hot Seat

✓ What are your three biggest fears about starting your own business?

✓ Give some examples of fears you have that may be healthy for you as an entrepreneur.

✓ Do you have a "Compelling Vision"?

✓ Will your vision be strong enough to keep you motivated as you work towards having your own business? Why?

STAND IN THE HEAT
Chapter Three

Staying Cool under Pressure

"Pressure is when you play for five dollars a hole with only two in your pocket."

- Lee Trevino
Professional golfer

The ability to stand in the heat and maintain composure is the mark of a champion in any field. Whether on the football field, the battlefield, or in the boardroom, those who can keep their wits about themselves and manage their emotions the best will most likely prevail. Imagine a three-foot putt on the 72nd hole to win the Masters. How many of us would have enough mental toughness to keep our emotions under control and sink the putt?

Over the past couple of years my wife and I have experienced our share of financial pressure. Financial pressure is one of the most intense and stressful types of pressure. It is probably responsible for the failure of more marriages than any other issue. My personal strategy for handling financial pressure is to remind myself that "It's ONLY money!" Money comes and goes and it always will. Fortunately, there is a massive amount of money in circulation and all we have to do is add more value to the marketplace to bring more our way.

The problem occurs when we have our identity too closely attached to our financial worth instead of our worth as a human being. Whenever you hear the tragic story of someone taking their life over money issues, it's a case of that person too closely associating their value as a human being with their net worth. Let's face it, if you have your health and a few good relationships in your life, everything else is gravy on the biscuit.

Understanding the symbiotic loop between our mind and our emotions is critical for staying cool under pressure. As you will learn from the folks in this chapter, there are strategies that we can employ with our physical body that directly impact the way we think and therefore the way we feel emotionally. I have always been a huge fan of the belief that "motion creates emotion." Our behavior can directly affect our attitude. Given this truth, I have always been one to *intentionally* wear a big smile and walk quickly and with purpose. There is no better strategy that I am aware of to immediately change your emotions than a deep breath, a big smile, and a walk down the hall like you own the world!

Willingness to Assume Risk

By nature, entrepreneurs need to be risk-takers. Whether it's in financial decisions, launching a new service, or changing established methods, there will be times you'll be taking a chance. George McKerrow, founder of LongHorn Steakhouse, says for starters, it's not as glamorous as it sounds. "You have to be willing to risk everything. I think it's a combination of self esteem, self-actualization, risk and reward. You must be willing to say to yourself, "You know what? If I don't try I'll never succeed."

Business Failure vs. Personal Failure

But, you have to have enough confidence that if you fail in business, you won't consider yourself a failure in life, George says. "I think too many times people equate the failure of an attempt to be successful in a business with failure in life. I didn't equate the success of LongHorn with the success of my inner self."

Growing or Dying

Brad Sugars, founder of ActionCOACH, a business coaching firm, believes that the average entrepreneur can stand in the heat if they're equipped with knowledge. "It's no more complex than that. If you know what you're doing then it doesn't matter how hot it gets in the kitchen. The only time when the heat gets too hot is when you sit down and go 'Hmm, I'm not sure if I'm doing the right thing,' or 'I don't even know what I'm doing.'" Brad says the moment you realize you don't know what you're doing you need to turn to someone for help. "A business has to be growing. If a business isn't growing it's dying. You've got to make sure that you're growing the business."

"If you knew it was going to be this hard..."

How many times have you heard someone say "If I had known..."? Hindsight is, and will always be, 20/20! If you haven't leapt into starting your own venture, why not? Are you always thinking about how hard it might be? Dave Liniger says ignorance is bliss. "If I had any idea how tough it was going to be initially I probably wouldn't have tried it. I had no idea what the obstacles were going to be. I just thought I was going to start a company just like other people start companies."

Within a couple of years of launching RE/MAX, Liniger said it was obvious that they were having financial problems. But they never even considered bankruptcy. "Bankruptcy was not to my moral standards." When the bills really began to overwhelm them, Dave's wife, Gail, took action. Gail told Dave that they couldn't get out of financial trouble if Dave spent all his time handling bill collectors. So she told him to recruit agents for RE/MAX while she kept bill collectors at bay. Gail was totally honest with the bill collectors. "It was Gail's negotiating ability and her forthright approach that the creditors appreciated. They didn't want to push us out of business. They just wanted to be paid," Dave says.

Gail's strategy got them to the point where they could break even. It took time to pay off their creditors, but Dave says many of those vendors stayed with them. "They didn't holler and scream or call us bad people. They just wanted to be paid. Several of them that stayed with us eventually became suppliers to the entire RE/MAX network and made an absolute fortune."

Looking back, Dave says there are a few things that he and Gail did really well. "First, we were very transparent with the agents. We flat out told them, 'This is how much we owe, and how much it is to each person.' We had five pages of yellow legal sized paper listing whom we owed money. 'This is 100 percent of what we owe.' They appreciated the transparency."

Another thing they did well was to always maintain a trust account for the agents' commissions. "No matter how bad my finances were, the agent always knew they would get paid. I would hand them a deposit slip for the commission account and they got their commission. I never missed a payroll for anybody." And finally, Dave says they always made sure to ask for the agents' input when they weren't sure what they were doing. "It built trust and cohesiveness."

Hot Thought

> *Play your course. Don't worry about the competition.*

Play Your Own Game

In the first chapter, our entrepreneurs shared their thoughts on being called crazy, and how despite what others thought, they went ahead with their plans. That focus on your goals can help you in trying to keep calm under pressure. Don't worry about what others are thinking, or what they're doing. This method works for restaurateur Pano Karatassos. "I don't necessarily worry about the competition as much as realizing that I'm my own competitor and I certainly have to become better every day."

Pano says his team works together to be better. "I've been fortunate that I've got a lot of people around me that have that pride and that passion. We have about two thousand of those in our company." They are no longer a small operation, but Pano still likes to think of them as a small family operation. This mentality of focusing on, and taking pride in, what they're doing has helped the company survive tougher economic times. "We're in the nickel-and-dime business and we have to watch our expenses no matter how small. During the tough times, you get together with your staff and let them know that, look, "If we're going to survive we're gonna survive this together."

Think Before You React

We've all done it, reacted a little too quickly. Maybe it's an email you should have let sit for a while before sending, or a response in a job interview that you wish you could take back right after you say it. By not reacting quickly, you may be able to help yourself stay cool in high-pressure situations. It works for Herman Cain: "Think before you react. Give yourself time to think," he says.

Give your brain time to try and process the situation you're in. If you react first you're being driven by your emotions. Herman says if you stop and think first, "You're being driven by your knowledge, your experience, your common sense. Reactionary emotion is a barrier to common sense and logical thinking."

Hot Thought

Spend time in the "Gap."

Compartmentalize Your Emotions

Factoring strong emotions into our decisions and actions is human nature. So how can we move past our gut instinct to keep our emotions in check? Learn to compartmentalize those emotions.

Heather Thomson calls it her "emotional backpack." "I put it on when I have to put it on, and it's heavy and it's painful, and it's ugly. And when I'm done with it for that day, I take it off and put it in the corner, I forget about and I keep it moving." Maidenform sued Heather's company to invalidate her patents. Her company countersued for patent infringement.

"They sued me because they felt my patents should not have filed." It was not an easy battle for Thomson to go through, and certainly one that was emotionally difficult for her, after all she had gone through to launch her shaping apparel line, Yummie by Heather Thomson. "Building a business is one thing. Having an original idea that you have to protect is another," she says.

"Maidenform is a much larger company with significantly more resources available to continue this lawsuit."

Ultimately, Maidenform paid Yummie by Heather Thomson a $6.75 million dollar settlement in 2011. Thomson says she not only learned a lot about the U.S. legal and judicial systems but moreover how to keep her emotions in check from this experience.

Never Let Your Fear Control You

Heather Thompson's shapewear company had to go up against a lawsuit from a major company, but Heather did her best to keep her emotions, and her fear, in check. That's Mo Anderson's strategy for staying cool when the heat is on. "It doesn't mean you're never afraid, but it means the fear doesn't control you," she says. "That, and knowing that there's light at the end of the tunnel. Going through the tough stuff develops character and builds stamina."

Fear of What May Never Come to Pass

If your fears have kept you from starting a business, how can you learn to control them? First, take a step back and examine each thing that worries you, and determine if they are legitimate fears. If they're not likely to ever present an issue, how do you keep them from holding you back? "I remember 99.9 percent of things that we fear never even happen so why bother?" says Joyce Bone. Joyce used to be afraid of alligators when she was little. In bed at night, she was afraid to put her feet on the floor and then go to the bathroom because she thought there was an alligator down there. "Obviously alligators don't live under four-year-olds' beds. I had myself so psyched out I didn't want to go to the bathroom, so that's silly. And I try to remember that as an adult."

Joyce says when your mind is fearful it can be like a magnet. "You're drawing trouble to yourself because you're focusing on what could happen instead of focusing on the work that you should be doing to make sure that it doesn't happen."

Hot Thought

> *"We become what we think about all day long."*
> - Ralph Waldo Emerson

Breathing

For Trish McCarty, her technique for controlling fear is as much physical as mental. She has learned ways to calm herself down. Trish, who comes from a strong corporate and banking background, opened a school for high-risk, inner-city children in Phoenix in 2002, called StarShine Academy. She faced obstacles in trying to open the school, but knew some tricks to help stay calm through the process.

When she was growing up, her father had a lot of heart problems. Trish would read lots of material on health and well-being, and in college she studied biology and took many medical courses. It led her to realize that the medical industry didn't have all the answers. "I became my own health expert and got very involved in doing yoga." After a two-year certification program, she began teaching yoga. "I started learning a lot of things about how to get through really tight spots as an executive, so I would be the CEO of a bank and on Saturday I'd go teach a class of yoga."

Through the yoga, she learned ways to control her breathing. Such as, "If you stand on one foot it triggers a muscle around your belly button—and that muscle is also the one that triggers "fight or flight"—so when you're standing on one foot and you're breathing slowly it shuts down your limbic brain." The limbic system is the part of the brain that is involved in motivation and emotional behaviors. Trish says they teach this method to the children at the Academy. "If they're getting ready to take a test, stand on one foot and breathe for thirty seconds, sixty seconds. It'll stop the limbic so that they can think straight." Ready to try it for yourself? I thought so!

Control Your Physiology

For some it's about controlling more than just breathing. Scott Goodknight shared a story with me about a time he was under pressure and stood in the heat.

When Scott was in the Rangers he was stationed in the jungles of Panama. As part of a training exercise, his squad was guarding a radio tower, and was anticipating an attack. One of the guys on his squad was collecting old used grenade simulators. "They're packed with black powder but there's no metal so they're not going to explode and shoot out shards and hurt anyone, but they were extremely loud and powerful and dangerous," says Scott. The guy was cutting them open and emptying out all the black powder into a pile. Scott told the guy he didn't think it was a good idea. "I mean, we're Rangers. Rangers are going to be Rangers. They're going to do dangerous things," says Scott.

The squad had been up for days with no sleep. Scott says he went to lay in the shade, when suddenly he heard a loud sound, "And then the next sound I heard is a sound I don't ever want to hear again and it was the sound—it sounded like a little girl screaming." Scott turned and saw a big puff of smoke, and the buddy who had been playing around with the black powder stumbling backwards. His eyes were wide open and his skin was all burnt up. "Literally skin is falling off of his face onto the ground and his arms, and his uniform is on fire and we ran over there and tackled him and, put him out basically. And now he's going into shock."

They couldn't get through to anyone using their radio, so Scott pulled out a map to look for the nearest aide station. As the other men were trying to help their injured squad member, Scott made the decision that one of them would have to run to the station for help. Time was running out. "If we didn't get him out of there soon he could go into shock and he could die." Knowing that he was the fastest runner in their group, Scott took off. "I ran as fast I think as I've ever run before in my life. I got to the aide station. It was like I had a GPS inside me. My own conscious mind was totally tuned. It knew the destination and it was like there was a homing beacon in me; it took me right to the aide station." He made it there; they got the medevac, and they were able to save the man's life.

HEAT Moment

Scott Goodknight took massive Action when he sprinted through the jungle to save his comrade's life.

Scott says he's had that instinct in other situations before. "There's this internal GPS that we all have that's connected to everything, to all living things and all. It's energy." He had belief in his ability to carry out the task. "I knew the terrain. I had some belief in myself. I was in the right emotional state. I was not in fear. I was not panicking. I had control of my body and my breathing."

Scott teaches fire walking, and says if you control your eye movements, your breathing, your facial expression and the words you're saying (out loud and to yourself) then you'll be in an emotional state of certainty no matter what's going on around you. "When people come to the fire walk they're looking down. I snap my fingers and I say 'Look up. Take a few deep breaths; get a certain look on your face. If you were absolutely certain you could do anything, what kind of look would you have on your face?'" Scott says you can see the see the shift happen.

If you're afraid, you're expressing that on your face, in your voice, and in your breathing and your body language. "Your family, your co-workers, and everybody else, they're going to pick up on it too." Scott says this will lead to everyone getting paralyzed and not taking action. "Belief is half of being. And you have to act as if it doesn't matter what's going on around. Just act as if you're under control—you're in control."

Hot Seat

✓ Think of a time where you reacted before thinking. Looking back, what would you have done differently?

✓ Do you have a technique you have used in the past to stay cool under pressure? What is it?

✓ Think of one new thing you can do to keep a level head when in tough situations.

✓ Are any of your fears things that may never come to pass?

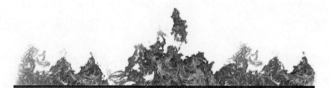

STAND IN THE HEAT
Chapter Four

Quitting Is Not an Option

"Never give in, never give in, never, never, never, never – in nothing, great or small, large or petty— never give in except to convictions of honour and good sense. Never yield to force; never yield to the apparently overwhelming might of the enemy."

- Winston Churchill

In many instances in life, the "overwhelming might of the enemy" can be our own thinking mind. The four inches between our ears can be the most frightening real estate on Earth. If I were to be completely transparent with you, I would admit that writing this book has been very challenging, from a belief and a discipline standpoint. Am I good enough to write a compelling book? Will this book hit the mark and be a success? Do I have the discipline to balance this project with a family and a full-time job? Many start-ups require that we ride two horses in the beginning to ensure that the bills are paid while we pursue our dream.

Entrepreneurship requires tremendous commitment, focus, discipline, and faith. Quitting and entrepreneurship are mutually exclusive. They are an emulsion of oil and water. They don't mix. Of all the successful entrepreneurs I have met and interviewed, none of them had the word "quit" in their vocabulary. It's never an option!

If you are like me, your ship has probably not come in on *your* timeframe. One of my favorite quotes is by Woody Allen. He once said, "If you want to make God laugh, tell him your plans." To me that quote speaks to timeframe. It has been my professional experience that most new ideas and business ventures take much longer and require more capital than originally expected. As a matter of fact, the number one reason most new businesses fail is due to lack of capital.

Hot Thought

Rarely do things come to pass on our time frame.

To be a successful entrepreneur, you cannot let **anything** get in your way. You can have excuses or results, but you cannot have both. Personally, I thought that I would have been a lot more successful at a much younger age. At forty-five years old, I still tend to beat myself up about where I am and where I think I should be. Thank God I have extremely supportive friends and family who constantly remind me that I am *exactly* where I am supposed to be. Although I get rather frustrated on a regular basis, I know that I will never quit nor give up on my dream. Don't you ever give up on yours!

Quitting Can't Be in Your DNA

Maybe you've felt it. There's something that makes an entrepreneur, or a soon-to-be entrepreneur, different from others. Could it be something in their DNA or maybe that something is *missing* from their DNA? George McKerrow thinks so. "Quitting was never an option for me. Quitting isn't in my DNA." When you read George's story, you'll see what he means.

A Risky Venture

McKerrow says the first nine months of starting up LongHorn Steakhouse were terrible. They needed $150,000 to build the first restaurant. He set up a first meeting with a bank. "My banker said, 'Ninety-five percent of all restaurants fail in the first year. I've looked at your business plan. Of all the restaurant plans I've seen, you seem to have a pretty good plan.'" The banker told him that they didn't finance restaurants, but were willing to loan him $0.70 on the dollar, or $70,000. At sixteen percent interest!

Next they went to the accountants, who said that ninety-five percent of all restaurants fail. But, they said the business plan was good, and that George knew what he was doing, so he could reasonably pull it off! Next were the lawyers, and then "that's where a fatal thing happened," says George. They had an original partner who had invested $30,000, and wanted out. "We agreed to buy him out for $15,000 over three years. He's lucky he got any of his money back." At the time, George and his father owned fifty-four percent of the company. It proved to be much better than if they were all equal partners with twenty-five percent each. They went to lawyers and drew up documents. "We all agreed what color Mercedes-Benz we were going to get when we were successful. Bingo. The company was formed. So, it went bankrupt before it ever opened."

George had two times where he could have easily walked away from the venture. But he stayed true to his vision and didn't quit, even when faced with being broke before they even opened that first restaurant!

When the Heat Becomes Flames

Pano Karatassos has had a lot of fortune in his life. But when times were really bad, he kept pushing forward and didn't let his determination falter. His father-in-law had helped set him up in a drive-in restaurant. Within the first couple of weeks it caught on fire twice and burned down to the ground. That fire was actually a blessing because it led Pano to his next venture where he eventually became Executive Chef of Hotel DeSoto. "That was the best thing, obviously, that happened to me," Pano says. "Two fires in four days! The restaurant was gone."

Pano says he used to go to work afraid every day. Afraid, because he wanted to do a better job every day. "I had that need, that urge, that want to be the best and I thought that I would be successful if I could attract people that had that same need, that want to be the best. Put that combination together we're all succeeding."

HEAT Moment

> *Pano displayed Tenacity in the face of fire and fear. He managed his emotions like a champion and went on to build an empire.*

Hire People to Do What You Cannot

When Trish McCarty was trying to set up StarShine Academy, she ran into roadblocks from someone who didn't think she should be in the education field. Trish tried for three years to file for a charter for the school. She said they kept turning her down. "Because the first gal who I handed the charter to said I didn't belong in education. She was going to do everything that she could to keep me out of it and that was a person that was one of the people involved in approving charters." Later, Trish found out that person had tried to open a charter school and it failed.

"She said to me, 'What makes you think you know anything about education; you're from business.' And I said, 'I can hire those people.' So, I took all of my own money because I couldn't get state money, couldn't get federal money because I wasn't a charter yet. So I maxed out three $10,000 credit cards and took all the money out of my 401(k) plan."

HEAT Moment

> *Trish McCarty exercised Tenacity when she didn't let a narrow-minded employee steal her dream of founding a charter school.*

Adopt the "Ranger Standard"

Scott Goodknight has the benefit of having an attitude cultivated by his time as a US Army Ranger. "There's several things about the Rangers that are different than any other elite fighting force out there. The main thing is the attitude. We used to call it the 'Ranger standard.' There was Army standards and then there were Ranger standards." Scott says the Rangers kept their equipment cleaner, dressed neater, and kept in better shape. "We just had the attitude of no matter what it takes, we're gonna get the job done. And you're never going to leave anybody behind no matter what; you're going to get the mission done no matter how hard it is. We knew what we were volunteering for. We knew what the odds were." Scott says Rangers always know that something bad can happen on a mission or even in training. He knows plenty of people who were injured or even killed in a training exercise. "It's the willingness; it's the desire to be in the best of the best. It's going to be tough and start taking pride in that."

Hot Thought

> *Most worthwhile accomplishments in life require that we stand in the* HEAT.

Scott's advice to anyone hoping to start their own business is this: "Volunteer yourself to catch the American spirit of being an entrepreneur and just don't give up no matter what. It's going to be hard. That's what you should take pride in."

Bad News Puts You in Check

Heather Thomson has learned the hard way that sometimes you'll have to fight to protect your work. When she got the news that Maidenform was suing her company, Yummie by Heather Thomson, she was in the car with her two children. She pulled over while her partner told her the bad news. "When I hung up the phone I got so emotional and I started to cry and Jackson and Ella said to me, 'Mommy what's wrong?' And I said, 'Somebody is trying to steal Yummie Tummie from mommy.' And that's how I felt about it."

She wiped away her tears, put the car back in drive, and while looking in the rear view mirror remembered that what was really important to her was right there in her back seat. "And that's all that mattered and it kind of puts you in check every day. And so I'll fight the fight. I'll fight the fight as long and as hard as I can fight it. And, you know, I'm not a quitter, but if it ever comes to a point where it's going to be detrimental to the business I will give up."

While bad news about your business can be devastating, try to remember the other things you have in your life that can help keep your perspective in check. Remember that there will be a lesson you can take away from the experience to help keep you moving forward.

Stick to Your Guns

I am greatly inspired by the story of Sylvester Stallone. Many people don't realize that he wrote the screenplay for the movie *Rocky*. His dream was to get the movie produced and star in it himself. When he first began shopping the movie to potential producers, he was completely broke. He was so broke that he almost had to sell his dog because he could barely afford to feed him. Eventually, Stallone found a producer to buy his movie, but didn't want him in the lead role. Imagine how he must have felt? He was starving and finally found someone to produce his first film. However, the producer didn't want Stallone to star in his own movie.

So, what did he do? He said "Next!" He found another producer willing to buy the film, but who didn't want Stallone in the lead role. Can you imagine the frustration? What would you have done in that position? He kept getting bigger and bigger offers for his film, but kept getting turned down for the lead role. What if he had sold out because he desperately needed the money? Where would he be today?

Hot Seat

✓ What's in your DNA that could make you a successful entrepreneur?

✓ What's missing from your DNA that sets you apart?

✓ If you were in George's situation of not getting the bank financing you were hoping for, and then having to buy out an investor, what would you do? Would you have quit or kept on going?

STAND IN THE HEAT
Chapter Five

Personal Tragedy

"Tragedy is a tool for the living to gain wisdom, not a guide by which to live."

- Robert F. Kennedy

Fortunately, I have never directly experienced personal tragedy. The closest thing to tragedy that I have experienced in my life was when my uncle David Carver, United States Air Force pilot, was killed when his C-130 crashed into a mountain in Tennessee in 1980. I remember the day that our family got the call like it was yesterday. It was surreal. It couldn't be true.

Uncle Dave was like a second father to me and he was one of the coolest guys on the planet. He taught me how to ride a motorcycle and he had a massive passion for music that greatly inspired me. He was a very large influence in my formative years. My wife and I have a spiritually gifted friend who believes that Uncle Dave is one of my son's Guardian Angels.

Some of the great entrepreneurs I have had the privilege to interview have experienced significant, personal tragedy. They used their tragedy to strengthen their resolve and further commit to their business and life mission. As Friedrich Nietzsche said, "That which does not kill us makes us stronger."

Tragedy Can Kill Your Spirit or Make You Stronger

Dr. Kathleen Hall helps others overcome tragedies and stress, as the founder of The Stress Institute and The Mindful Living Network. Dr. Hall herself can speak from firsthand experience about the effects of tragedy, having had a near-death experience. She was in Beverly Hills for a meeting with her business partner, to discuss plans for some television programs. She stepped off a curb to cross the street, and was hit by a woman who was going about forty-five miles per hour.

"I was dead for about five minutes," she says. Dr. Hall was taken to the trauma unit at Cedars-Sinai hospital. She had suffered a traumatic brain injury, broken ribs on her left side, a broken hip. She was flown back to Atlanta for after-care. Doctors had to give her a tremendous amount of donor blood.

"When I got healthy again, every African-American I saw, every Muslim I saw, every homeless person on a corner I saw—I'd go up and want to kiss them and go, 'Guess what, I think I have your blood—you saved my life!'" She says she went around kissing people for a month. "My husband finally said, 'You have to stop this crap honey. It's going to take us two years to get through Publix!'"

Hot Thought

Regardless of race, religion, or politics, we are ultimately all the same.

Dr. Hall says before the accident she was quite the media girl, appearing on CNN regularly. "And all that stopped, my life stopped. I questioned my life a lot. Then the next year still recuperating and very much going back inside of myself saying, 'What am I supposed to do? What direction?'" She says she began listing to her friends and looking at the world. "Wall Street, finances crumbling, home foreclosures . . . and I went, 'You know what, it was never supposed to be just about a television network.' That was so narrow."

The silver lining in that accident came when she realized that what she had been teaching, and what she had learned in her formal education and training, worked! After her recovery, Dr. Hall became a wellness educator and took over a cardiac rehab program. "When people have zippers and have had their chest open and their hearts either replaced or repaired or they have a woman who comes in with no breasts in my cancer group, they don't want one more prescription. It's like 'I can't take one more thing from a doctor or somebody medical to tell me to do.' So what I figured was it had to have spiritual meaning for them."

HEAT Moment

> *Dr. Kathleen Hall exemplified Tenacity when she survived a near death experience and redefined the Mindful Living Network.*

Stay Focused During Challenging Times

Dr. Hall's accident made her feel like she had lost her sense of direction. But during her recovery, she regained her strength and set her life on a new path. It's easy for challenges to make us feel like we've lost our way, or can't stay on track to accomplish our goal, whether it's achieving a sales record, opening a new business, or filing a patent.

So how can we keep our focus? For Mo Anderson, her road to entrepreneurial success wasn't smooth sailing. "It was a very bumpy road, both personally and professionally," she says. "My sister was in a hospital here dying of Leukemia and here I was trying to open my first Keller Williams market center. And then I sold a franchise and opened that market center. She ultimately died about three months after I opened it, so it was hard." Mo says not only was it difficult on a personal level, it was also hard from a business perspective. "People clearly didn't understand this very novel business model." But with all that was happening in her life, Mo was strong enough to stay focused on her goal of building Keller Williams. Her focus and strength have paid off—today Keller Williams has not just one, but almost seven hundred market centers across the United States and Canada.

Tragedy Can Embolden Your Courage

They say that beside every great man walks a great woman. For Dave Liniger, seeing his wife's courage after she survived a plane crash was inspirational.

Gail and Dave were in a small town outside of Toronto for a RE/MAX convention. One afternoon, one of the franchisees offered to give Gail a ride in his C-plane. She and two other officers went for a ride in the plane. "Unfortunately, the pilot crashed and he died, and Gail ended up in the hospital in a coma," Dave says. Gail began to recover, but her recovery was very slow. She was hospital-bound for at least six months. When Gail left the hospital, she used a cane and supporting casts, but left on her own power.

Gail showed remarkable courage during her recovery. "She never looked back and she never cried. She never voiced that, 'This isn't fair. I've got paralysis on my left side. I can't drive. I can't this or that.'" The annual RE/MAX convention was in Orlando, Florida that year. When Gail was wheeled onto the stage on opening day, with her head shaved on one side, smiling, the crowd cheered and cried. "Her personal courage was an inspiration for an awful lot of people."

Focus on That Which You Can Control

"Adversity allowed me to figure out that I was an entrepreneur," Heather Thomson, creator of the Yummie shapewear line, tells me. Her first child, Jackson, was born ill. "At birth, he wasn't breathing. His first forty-eight hours of life were really touch and go. We didn't know if he was going to make it or not." Then, at just three months old, Jackson was diagnosed with a rare liver disease called biliary atresia. He needed a liver transplant to survive. At six months old, he underwent a liver transplant. Heather says she put on weight during this difficult time. "I gained about sixty-five pounds. And I ate like a pig and I deserved to gain sixty-five pounds. For the first time in my life I was really hit with a weight loss quandary."

At the time, Heather was focused solely on her child. She was working for superstar Beyonce Knowles at the time and Beyonce and her mother were very supportive of Heather and her family. Heather says at one point they encouraged her to come into the office to visit. "They were worried that maybe my child wouldn't live and I wouldn't have any normalcy, and so they encouraged me to come into work and just hang with some people for a few hours." She decided to make the visit. "I knew I could hold it together from a mental and emotional standpoint, but from a physical standpoint I wasn't the person they were used to seeing. I didn't want to go into work and have people feel sorry for me, so I went to the shapewear department to boost my confidence." Heather knew she couldn't control the issues with her son's health, but she could get some garments that would help her feel better about going in to visit friends.

So she went to the shapewear department to try to boost her confidence, but instead found choices that not only failed aesthetically but also functionally. And so the idea for the first Yummie product was born. "It really came out of my own personal need, the brand. It was literally with a tear streaming down my face that I sewed the first Yummie Tummie tank at my own dining room table." And the rest is shapewear history.

HEAT Moment

Heather Thomson took Action and turned an incredible adversity into opportunity when she started her company based on a personal need.

Hot Seat

✓ Think back to an extremely difficult time in your life. Did you feel like you lost your way for a time? What helped you find your focus again?

✓ List three things you can control if you're facing tragedy or adversity in your life.

✓ Is there someone who has suffered an accident or illness, or overcame difficult odds, who inspires you? What qualities of theirs do you admire the most? Do you see yourself adopting any of those qualities?

STAND IN THE HEAT
Chapter Six

The Best and Worst of Entrepreneurship

"An entrepreneur tends to bite off a little more than he can chew hoping he'll quickly learn how to chew it."

- Roy Ash
Co-founder and President of Litton Industries

A friend of mine has a very similar philosophy to Roy Ash when it comes to business. My friend used to say, "Bite off more than you can chew and frickin' chew it!" Sometimes it can be a good strategy to set a "trap" for ourselves that forces us to do specific behavior.

It has been said that the best thing and the worst thing about being an entrepreneur is the same thing—the fact that we are our own boss. Most people who have the drive and determination to become an entrepreneur still need accountability and discipline. The major difference between people who have what they want and people who don't have what they want is the willingness to do the things they don't want to do in order to have the things they want.

Personally, I struggle with discipline and head trash on a regular basis. I suppose it's the human condition. Writing this book has been a challenging experience for me. I am confident that most entrepreneurs struggle with the same issues and constantly ask themselves the same nagging questions. "Am I really good enough?" "Am I smart enough?" "Am I starting too late?" "Who am I to think I can pull this venture off?" And the really big question: "What if I go for my dream and fail? Where will I be then?"

Hot Thought

> *What would you attempt if you were convinced you would succeed?*

It is critical for entrepreneurs to keep their demons at bay. The thinking mind can be our greatest asset and simultaneously be our greatest adversary. I study NLP (neuro-linguistic programming) on a regular basis in order to keep my mind and emotions in alignment. I have found over the years that the most successful people in life have coaches and accountability partners. As much as I have resisted accountability at times in my life, I have come to fully embrace and appreciate my need for accountability.

I have also come to realize that I am more motivated by self-imposed consequences of my behavior than self-imposed rewards. Huh? Psychologists tell us that we will do more to avoid pain than gain pleasure. Entrepreneurship can oftentimes be a lonely road without support or guidance. I have found it to be extremely effective to use a combination of the proverbial "carrot and stick."

It has been said that when your "Why" is strong enough, the rest will fall into place. Obviously, you have a big "Why" or you wouldn't be reading this book. So, take a big bite my friend, get a coach who holds you accountable and chew, chew, chew!

Freedom

I asked these entrepreneurs what was the best and worst thing about being in business for themselves. Herman Cain gave me what is probably my favorite answer. "The best thing about being an entrepreneur is the freedom that goes with it. The worst thing about being an entrepreneur is the freedom that goes with it." He calls entrepreneurship a double-edged sword. "The liberties you have are much better than the challenge of the other side of it, because you know it's going to cost you something. There's a price you have to pay for it."

Sometimes you can be so focused on the positive aspects of starting your own business or getting your idea off the ground (Who doesn't want to set their own hours, or wear sweats at your home office?), that you forget about the "other" stuff that makes up the whole picture. And that "other" stuff can be many different things, including investors, start-up expenses, maintenance costs, staffing, applications for permits or licensing . . . the list goes on and on.

Your Customers are Your Boss

One of those things that most don't think about when hoping to become an entrepreneur, says Herman Cain, is who is really in charge? "You've probably heard some people say, 'Well one day I want to have my own business so I can be my own boss.' Well I've got a breaking news announcement for you: If you have your own business your customers are your boss!"

It's like that old saying, "The customer is always right." Your customers will end up "telling" you what to do regardless of what type of industry you're in. It could be what hours to keep, what prices to charge, what merchandise or services you should offer, even whether or not you should change the décor or re-design your logo. And while in some ways it will be a positive for you to have all these "bosses," in other ways it could make you question your decision to start your own business!

Hot Thought

Like it or not,
we ALL have a boss.

Risk and Reward

For restaurateur Pano Karatassos, his customers are most definitely his boss. But that is not the most difficult part for him in being an entrepreneur. "The most difficult part is the financial risk. And doing a better job each day," he says. Pano says it takes people to help you accomplish that. "I was fortunate and had a great group of people that grew with me, and I helped grow their careers . . . launched some of them in their own businesses." Without that great group, it may have been a little rough in the beginning. "For a while, I used to come to work every day scared," Pano says. When launching your service or business, you need to have a team of people that you trust around you. Not just as staff you might have around you, or investors, but a support network that is there for you as you take the risks of entrepreneurship, and hopefully reap the rewards.

Balance

The average entrepreneur is a go-getter. They have a goal and a plan and they are determined to "get there." And once they're "there" they keep going, just like Yummie founder Heather Thomson. "You know, that's where my friends call me crazy. I just never stop." That drive, she says, is the best and worst thing about having her own business. "I never stop working; there's never enough hours in the day to get the job done." For Heather, it has been hard at times to balance her drive in her professional life with her personal life. But she has learned to find that balance as her children have gotten older. "When they were infants it was easy because when they need you, they need you and nothing waits. But when they're two you can say 'Hold on a second.'"

She's grateful for her smartphone, which gives her an ability to allow one aspect of her life to overlap with the other, but at the same time, "Sometimes my kids think it's actually a part of my body," she says. But she has one firm rule when she goes home to her family at night. "I never have my cell phone on my head or in my hand or visible at all. I walk in the door as mom. And I stay that way until they go to bed and then I fire it back up again. And I work as long as I need to."

Mo Anderson says she was fortunate that her kids were grown and out of the house when she began to develop her entrepreneurial path. "I think the worst thing about being an entrepreneur is that you do have to go through those periods of time where there's absolutely no balance. It's that price you have to pay," she says. Mo says that some people have to pay a price with her family. I think many of us can relate to that statement. In working on this book, there are many times I felt like it was taking away from time with my wife and son.

Hot Thought

In the beginning of your venture, expect a total lack of balance.

As she worked to grow Keller Williams Realty, Mo came to see what she thinks is the best thing about being an entrepreneur. "You know how you have absolutely affected the lives of so many people," she says. "In a small business it might only be four or five lives. In a large business it could be hundreds of thousands. There is no greater satisfaction to me than knowing that you provided people jobs, that you had an influence on their life for the better." Mo says that is the reason why the most important stated value at Keller Williams is this: "God and family first and the business second."

Hot Seat

✓ Imagine that you have started your dream business:

✓ What kind of freedom will it add to your life?

✓ What kind of risk will it add?

✓ What might some of the rewards be?

✓ Think of a time where you may have put work first and your loved ones second. Was it worth it? Would you do it again?

✓ Think of what is most important to you and your future venture. What might your company's stated value be?

Section II

Visualize Your Outcome

"Maybe we should try visualization, Chief!"

The first book I ever read twice as an adult is *You'll See It When You Believe It* by Dr. Wayne Dyer. What an amazing book! Dr. Dyer explains that we will rarely see something materialize in the physical world unless we believe it first. Think about your own life for a moment—and be honest with yourself. Whether your beliefs are positive or negative, evidence will surely present itself in the real world to support your beliefs. Why do we always see fans in the stadiums of championship games holding signs that say, "We Believe"? They are expressing their belief in the expectation that their victory will follow.

Be very careful what you think and don't believe everything you think. We human beings are creatures of habit and we are typically ruled by our subconscious programming. Unfortunately for most people, their subconscious has been programmed by others over a lifetime and it hasn't always been positive programming. If you don't take personal responsibility and program your mind, someone else certainly will!

In the early 1990s, I was first introduced to the concept of the "Pygmalion effect." It refers to the phenomenon in which the greater the expectation placed upon people, the better they perform. The Pygmalion effect is a form of self-fulfilling prophecy, in that we will internalize our positive visions and succeed accordingly. It suggests that we act as if we have already become the person that we want to become.

I love the example of how Jim Carrey took responsibility and clearly visualized the person he wanted to become. The story is told that one night in 1990 when Jim Carrey was a struggling young comic trying to make his way in Los Angeles, he drove his old beat-up Toyota to the top of a hill. While sitting there, broke, looking down over the city, and dreaming of his future, he wrote himself a check for $10 million, put in the notation line "for acting services rendered," and dated it for Thanksgiving 1995. He stuck that check in his wallet—and the rest, as they say, is history.

I believe most people never close the gap between where they are and where they want to be for two reasons. First, they are shut down by fear. Second, they never get absolutely crystal clear about what they really want. I will be the first to admit that I used to be one of these people. I used to hope, wish, and dream about creating my own brand as an author and speaker, but it didn't happen until I released my fear, developed a compelling mission and clearly visualized myself becoming the person I want to be.

STAND IN THE HEAT
Chapter Seven

Traits of a Successful Entrepreneur

"The important thing is not being afraid to take a chance. Remember, the greatest failure is to not try. Once you find something you love to do, be the best at doing it."

- Debbi Fields
Founder, Mrs. Fields Cookies

If there were one trait that I believe all successful entrepreneurs have in common, that trait would be the willingness to assume risk. By definition, an entrepreneur is "one who organizes, manages, and assumes the risks of a business or enterprise," usually with considerable initiative and risk.

In my personal and business life, I have always been willing to get out of my comfort zone and take on risk. Whether it is public speaking, jumping out of an airplane, or entering into a new business venture, I have always enjoyed stepping into the unknown. I learned many years ago that in business as in life, we are either growing or dying. And if we are comfortable, we are probably dying.

I remember reading a magazine article about Bill Gates back when Microsoft was on top of the world. He said that he woke up every morning and knew that he had to be running "Mach 4 with his hair on fire," lest he and Microsoft get run down by the competition. That comment really struck a chord in me. The great leaders in life, whether they are in sports, military, politics, or business, know that they can never get comfortable and rest on their laurels.

You may have heard this quote before. "Every morning in Africa, a gazelle wakes up. It knows it must outrun the fastest lion or it will be killed. Every morning in Africa, a lion wakes up. It knows it must run faster than the slowest gazelle, or it will starve. It doesn't matter whether you're a lion or gazelle—when the sun comes up, you'd better be running." Something tells me that Bill Gates had that quote plastered on his wall.

The biggest risk I ever took was in December 2003 when I packed up my car and drove to Phoenix, Arizona, with two nickels to my name to become a "roadie" for a great sales trainer named Paul Schween. I had been referred to Paul by a mutual friend and we hit it off immediately over the phone during an extended conversation. Paul was launching a seminar entitled "Selling Outside of the Box" and he needed someone to hit the road and help him sell tickets. I was immediately interested!

I have another good friend, Chip Eichelberger, who used to be an international "roadie" for Tony Robbins and I had always been extremely intrigued by that business model. I first met Chip in the late '90s in Atlanta during one of his free, one hour, promotional talks for Tony Robbins who was coming to town in the near future. He gave an outstanding preview of the upcoming seminar and sold tickets to the event.

Hot Thought

If you aren't running and growing, you're probably dying.

Paul Schween was looking for someone to do for him what Chip had done for Tony Robbins. After a couple considerable conversations, we determined that I was his man. We launched "Selling Outside of the Box" in Los Angeles in the spring of 2004. If you know anything about the speaking and training business, Los Angeles is the epicenter of the universe for competition in that industry. Everybody who is anybody is there.

We didn't get rich, but it was one of the best experiences of my life. Because I was willing to get out of my comfort zone and take a risk, I traveled down the corridor of public speaking which has ultimately led to the writing of this book. Take a risk my friends!

Self-Motivation

It's difficult to put your finger on that "special something" that makes entrepreneurs stand out. Herman Cain says there are not one, but three critical characteristics that an entrepreneur must have: the D, E, and F factor. The D factor is the Drucker factor, which refers to self-motivation. "You can't motivate people. People must motivate themselves," Herman says. The E factor is the entrepreneur factor, which Herman tells me is the risk factor. And then F factor is the ability to focus. Herman says the number one characteristic of successful entrepreneurs is the ability to focus. "When you're starting a business or you're trying to create a new concept, whatever the case may be, you've got to keep your eye on the prize. You've got to make sure that you don't get distracted and try too many things too fast or too little." Herman says that's how most entrepreneurs and business people get off track.

Hot Thought

*Ultimately, we must
motivate ourselves.*

When he took on the role of president and CEO of Godfather's Pizza, Herman felt that they were trying to do too much with too little, too fast. There were 725 restaurants at the time. He says they decided to get back to the basics. "Let's do what we're good at, let's focus on that, and let's work within our means to grow the business slowly rather than trying to grow it at warp speed," he says. "If you've got the resources to grow it fast and you've got the people to grow it fast go for it." But Herman says most businesses have a minimal amount of capital to get things going, they don't have the luxuries of trying to grow it fast. So in that case, take a slower approach. Focus on what you're best at, and work up from there.

Regardless of the D, E, and F factors, Herman believes there is ultimately one major trait difference between an entrepreneur and a non-entrepreneur. "Entrepreneurs are not afraid to fail."

Believe in Yourself

You have to believe in yourself and your ideas in order to do what it takes to make them happen. Lisa Levison says the thing that got her back on her feet was the trust that she could "get off that sidewalk and into that door." The derma-glove founder told me, "I have to trust me. I have to trust that my ideas are believable and that I am my biggest supporter." Lisa says this trust will train your brain to believe and get excited.

She says she can tell when someone has a great idea but they're just not feeling it. When it comes to her own career, she says, "I talk to myself about what I want to do. I believe what I want to do." Lisa is constantly setting her mind to the point that if she believes it, it will be attainable. But it's not something that she shares with others. "I work within myself to believe that it is believable. It's trust in me and it's trust in the concept and it's trust that I can do it." But for Lisa it's not about then trying to do everything on her own once she believes in it. "If I'm going to sell it to someone or ask someone to come in, I have to trust that they trust me and I want them to know that I trust them."

Sometimes once you have that trust, you still have to take the risk of "letting go" and hoping that something will grow. It could be in hiring a new member for your team, or putting a project into someone else's hands. "Letting go is taking a risk. I think any entrepreneur will tell you that what we do is we take a risk," Lisa says. She says take risks, but you need to have trust that you can control the end result. You have to have enough belief in your mission to see it through.

Weather the Heavy Storms

We're all born with different traits, whether they are physical, emotional, or mental. But how does one know if they have the traits of an entrepreneur? Trish McCarty says that when she was with AT&T, they used to put staff through tests to see what their natural instincts were, and what could be taught to them. She says that today her StarShine academy does similar testing with both kids and teachers.

So can a person who doesn't have the instincts of an entrepreneur be taught? Yes and no. Some traits just can't be taught. "You have to be able to weather a lot of really heavy storms in order to be an entrepreneur—it's not for the lighthearted," Trish says. Having that heart, she says, is instinctual. While some people have just fallen into making a lot of money and having a great idea, Trish says, "For most people I've ever met they've had huge failures, and it's through the failures that they've learned something else. There's something

78

inside of you that just keeps driving you forward when everything else is falling apart."

Hot Thought

We learn more from our failures than from our successes.

But since heart alone won't make or keep you successful, Trish says, you have to constantly learn to keep up with whatever is going on. She is always in "training mode," reading about five books a week and taking seminars. "I think everybody needs to be in that vein if they want to get ahead today."

Entrepreneurship is 24/7

Like Trish, be prepared for late nights and long hours as an entrepreneur. When you have your own business, you'll need to live and breathe it 24/7. "It's a rare night that I don't go to bed thinking about the business, thinking of what I can do tomorrow that will be better," says Pano Karatassos. Pano believes that an extremely hard work ethic and being hands-on are the number one traits that a successful entrepreneur in the restaurant industry has to have today. "There's just no substitute," he says. "To think that it's a lot easier to just put on a fancy suit every day and everything's going to be fine—it's not going to work." He says that the staff will expect you to be around. Or if they don't expect it, they will certainly appreciate the fact that you are around and that you work together with them to carry the load.

And it's not just helping with the workload, he says. There is a financial obligation he has to his staff. "They have their career goals as well and they have to feel comfortable with you that you can be a part of their growth and help them grow and become better professionals and providers for their families." In today's business world, Pano says an entrepreneur has to be well financed. He (or she) has to make sure that there is definitely a market for what they are doing and that they're not in business just for the sake of being in business. "Too many people have gotten hurt that way." He also believes that they need to be knowledgeable in the business that they are going into. "There's no getting by on a shoestring and expecting others to do it for you."

Confidence without Arrogance

Besides the ability to be willing to take a risk, another "must-have" trait for an entrepreneur is confidence. George McKerrow says his mother taught him as a young man to be confident without being arrogant. "She taught me to be self-assured but not overbearing. She also taught me to be a risk-taker." He says those characteristics are inherent in a successful entrepreneur. "I think you have to have a huge tolerance for risk. That tolerance can come from either naiveté or stubbornness. You have to be confident and want to take those risks." George says all the great entrepreneurs have those characteristics. He puts it to me this way, "If you're looking for security, predictability, and regular patterns in your life, then you probably won't succeed as an entrepreneur."

Hot Thought

Confidence attracts.
Arrogance repels.

Entrepreneurship and Security Are Mutually Exclusive

Can you have security and a guarantee of success if you're going to be an entrepreneur? It depends on why you want to be an entrepreneur. Are you motivated by money? "I've never been motivated by money. I'm still not motivated by money," George says. "I believe the most successful entrepreneurs generally want to be successful, but it isn't about money. The unsuccessful entrepreneurs are the ones who are after the money exclusively."

Commitment, Luck, and Sacrifices

Sometimes it takes just the right mix of factors to make a successful entrepreneur. What the business world needs, George says, are young people who have big entrepreneurial ideas, but can balance their plans with some sense of reality. And they might just need a little bit of luck!

"Being a successful entrepreneur takes commitment, but it also takes luck. Did luck play a part in my success? Absolutely. Was Ted (Turner) lucky? Absolutely. You have to be at the right place at the right time, but luck is always involved. However, the harder I work, the luckier I get!" He believes that success is a combination of timing, tempo, position, and luck. And, he says, most people don't realize how hard it is to be an entrepreneur. "I sacrificed my relationship with my wife and my first child for those dreams. When I look back, I realize that I was very singularly focused. I verged on being selfish, but you have to be. If you're not willing to make the sacrifices and do the hard work, you won't be a successful entrepreneur." In that case, he says, you're better off getting a job.

Hot Thought

> *Be willing to make*
> *sacrifices or keep your job.*

Control Your Fear

Joyce Bone stresses the need for persistence and commitment for those hoping to strike out on their own in business, to keep up with obstacles that are always going to be thrown at you. "Usually what happens is you get into something and all of a sudden you're in so deep you're like, 'Oh my gosh, what am I doing?' 'Oh, goodness, if I'd only known then what I know now would I have done this?'" She believes a lot of entrepreneurs find themselves in that position at some time or another. The ability to control your fear will allow you to stay committed to working towards your goal. "You have to be able to control your fear because that can just demobilize you in an instant," she says. "You have to be good at putting yourself on a mental diet on what you allow into your mind because you can easily get rattled."

Assume Calculated Risks

We're hearing all of our entrepreneurs say that you need to be a risk-taker. But you have to be careful about what risks you're taking. Your risks, Joyce says, must be calculated. "Sometimes entrepreneurs are kind of portrayed as foolhardy, but all the successful entrepreneurs I know take calculated risks, not stupid dumb risks." The successful ones take thought-out, researched risks, she says. "You don't win 100 percent of the time. If you do you're probably not trying hard enough." Joyce says you have to have a certain ability to bounce back, "skinned knees," she calls it. "You get knocked to the ground, skin your knees but they get back up and keep going and say, 'Yeah, that sucks but, I'm not dead. I can regroup and I'm going to keep marching forward.'"

Care about What You're Doing

Heather Thomson says the number one trait a successful entrepreneur has to have is drive. "You gotta want it. If you don't want it you're never gonna get it. You've gotta want it." But is there more to it than that? Thomson believes there is. "The key to success is you gotta care about what you're doing. I always say it's only work unless there's some place else you'd rather be. You know, it's not work to me. I love what I do. And I leave for my family, and I stop working for my family and my friends. . . but, a lot of my friends are designers and we talk about work and, you know, we talk about these things. My husband is a member of the board. I mean, I am my brand and my brand is me."

If you have a passion for something, you have an advantage, says Dave Liniger. "I think the most important ingredient for anybody considering the launch of a business is having an absolute passion for that business. If you've got the passion, you can sell the dream."

Patience and Persistence

Like George McKerrow, Wendy Reed also thinks there's a combination of traits that make up a successful entrepreneur. The number one for her? Courage. She says there are a lot of people who have a lot of ideas, but they just never go through with them. "I've had people say this to me: 'Oh that was my idea, I just never did it.' And I'd go, okay, well then it wasn't your idea. I mean, if you don't do it, it doesn't count." The other trait? "A combination of patience and persistence that I think needs to be balanced. You have to push, push, push but you have to bring people along as well which is where the patience comes in." If someone isn't seeing your vision, Wendy says, you have to have the patience to show it to them in pieces so that they get what you're trying to accomplish.

Honor Your Core Values

If you're an American entrepreneur, Scott Goodknight recommends you hold on to the core values the nation was founded on. "We came here looking to escape unfair taxes and tyrannical rule and just the stifling oppression of greedy and self-centered oppressors." It's in our blood, he says. "It was more important for us to have freedom and adventure and the possibility of huge, huge financial gain than it was security."

Scott believes that as Americans, we're taught through consumerism and mass marketing that we need to wear certain things, drive a certain type of car, or go on a certain type of vacation. "You're going to have to put that stuff aside for a while; don't worry about what people think," he says, if you want to be an entrepreneur. Scott tells me how Sam Walton, the founder of Walmart, was making millions, but he drove an old truck that was missing a passenger seat. (His hunting dog sat on the floor board.) All of Sam's managers got together and bought him a brand new truck. Well, he got angry and he said, "Take it back. I want my truck back. I want my old truck back."

Being an entrepreneur, Scott says, is about appreciating whatever is at your core. "If you like to wear blue jeans and t-shirts then create a business where you can wear blue jeans and t-shirts."

Be a Pioneer

Mo Anderson believes every entrepreneur has to have the spirit of being a pioneer. "It's that tenacity. It's moving forward when everything is against you," she says. Mo says she experienced that feeling of trying to walk upstream and learning tenaciousness while growing up as a tenant farmer's daughter. "We were very poor and I worked my way through college. That was totally upstream." she says. She is proof that you can work against the current and come out on the other side. "Everything I have ever done has been against all odds so it's a way of life for me. If it isn't tough it's probably not worth doing."

Willingness to Learn

Are you willing to be a lifelong learner? If so, you can be a successful entrepreneur. Brad Sugars says people often think that because they are good at something, that they will make a good business owner. "That's why most businesses that I see fail. It was just a lack of knowledge on the behalf of the business owner. I know the best thing for me that ever happened was I started my business very, very young so I wasn't old enough to believe I actually knew what I was doing. I was young enough and naïve enough to actually go and learn." Brad educated himself by reading, attending seminars, and taking advice from the right people.

"Learning by doing is the most costly layer of learning. There's two costs in life, one is time and the other is cash. A lot of people seem to think that oh well, time cost isn't that bad – I've got plenty of time. Well, no you don't really. You've only got one lifetime – eighty years, that's four thousand weeks so, if you're going to waste five years or two hundred fifty to two hundred sixty weeks on trial and error I'm not sure that's such a clever strategy."

And what are the things that drive Brad to continue to learn and grow in business? "Number one is doing a better job; doing what you can do better. Number two is invention and creation – I like creating new things and inventing new ways and strategies." And the third driving force for Brad is the people side of business: "Getting a great result with people, but also seeing people get the benefits of doing great work."

Hot Seat

- ✓ What traits do you have that you believe will make you a successful entrepreneur?

- ✓ What traits do you lack? Can you learn these?

- ✓ Do you consider yourself a risk-taker? List three things you are willing to risk to try to achieve your dreams.

- ✓ Why do you want to be an entrepreneur? Are you just "in it for the money"?

- ✓ How will your business or venture honor your core values?

- ✓ Are you ready to be a lifelong learner? Give some examples of how you can continue to try to learn and grow once you start your business.

STAND IN THE HEAT
Chapter Eight

Mentors

"If a man is to shed the light of the sun upon other men, he must first of all have it within himself."

- Romain Rolland
Nobel Laureate, Literature

I believe two things will separate you from where you are today and where you are five years from now – the books you read and the people with whom you associate. As entrepreneurs we must surround ourselves with great resources. Great resources come in the form of books, seminars, school, coaches, and ultimately mentors. Fortunately, your mentors can be living or deceased. I love reading about the lives and accomplishments of the great thinkers of the past. With the tremendous access to information that we have in our technology-rich world, we can learn from and be mentored by anyone in the past or present.

Looking back over my life I would say that I have had six mentors. My first mentor has and always will be my father. If you were to Google "never quit" you would absolutely be directed to a picture of my Dad. He is the eternal optimist and has the tenacity of a pit bull. His resilience never ceases to amaze me as he continues to reinvent himself in his seventies. Look out Colonel Sanders!

My second mentor has been one of my best friends in the world over the past twenty-five years. Michael McKeller (www.ExtremeMike.com) is the ultimate Ambassador of Attitude as he has been confined to an electric wheelchair since he was in his young teens. In spite of his *physical* disability, he is absolutely the most *mentally* tough man I have ever met in my life. He has *chosen* to take his limitations and turn them into a positive by inspiring other people to get out of their comfort zone and conquer their fear.

My third mentor was my little league football coach in Baltimore, Maryland. Coach Robert Sharbaugh gave me the greatest compliment of my life when I was a kid and it stays with me to this day: "You are the best *person* I have ever coached." His words echo in my mind when the doubt and little voices start to chatter. Never underestimate the power and long-term influence that your words can have on the life of a child.

My other mentors are three iconic authors, speakers, and influencers who continue to shape the thinking of the world today. I have been studying Dr. Wayne Dyer, Tony Robbins, and Stephen Covey for the past twenty years. Their philosophies about life, business, and relationships have guided and inspired me for two decades. When I read their words or listen to their voices, I truly feel as if I am standing on the shoulders of giants!

You Can Be Whatever You Want to Be

Many of us find mentors or even "heroes" when we are young. For some it may be a parent or a teacher. Herman Cain cites two people in addition to his father as his mentors. Dr. Benjamin Mays, the president of Morehouse College while Herman was attending school there, was someone that inspired him. "He walked the talk and he was always driven, he was always encouraging us to don't just do enough in life, do more than just enough in life. I'm paraphrasing some of his great speeches. I really admired Dr. Mays." Herman was in the 100th graduating class of the college, so in addition to encouragement from Dr. Mays, he says he felt an additional pressure on himself. "That was to not be satisfied with 'okay,' not to be satisfied with just getting the job done, but after you get the job done, to ask 'What's next?'" His other mentor was his high school math teacher, Mr. Charles S. Johnson. "Mr. Johnson instilled a spirit in me to compliment the spirit that I had from my dad and he summed it up this way — he used to say in his southern drawl, 'Herman Cain, you can be whatever you want to be. You might have to work a little harder. You might have to work a little longer, but you can be whatever you want to be.'"

Hot Thought

It might take you longer than expected, but you can be whatever you want to be.

Mo Anderson says her parents constantly told her when she was young, "When you grow up you have the ability to do anything you want to do." She calls this a "gift" from her parents. Mo's family lived in poverty, and she says her father taught her at a young age the difference between responsibility and entitlement. "He would say to us, 'We are not accepting a government handout. We are by our own initiative gonna figure out a way to pay these bills and get what we need.'" Mo says her father insisted that all five children work, and at six years old she had a cow she had to milk every morning before school. "The workload increased as I grew older and with him not allowing us to have a handout we developed an unbelievable work ethic. So I grew up not being afraid of work."

Does Every Entrepreneur Need a Coach?

Ironically, Brad Sugars doesn't think so. He says there are three "groups" of entrepreneurs when it comes to having a mentor or coach. "There's one group who I don't think should have a business coach and they're the ones that already know everything," he says. "If you already believe you know everything a coach will simply annoy. All they will be trying to do is help you grow the business."

Another group, Brad says, are those who need a coach now. "They know they need the coach now. They're willing to take the coach on and they go and do it." And the third group is made up of those who say, "I'll think about it." Brad says people in this group actually need a coach more than anyone else, but they're going to sit around and think about it. "If someone ever said to me, 'I don't think I need a business coach,' I would say,

'Give me the name and number of your competitor, I'll coach them.'"

Brad says about 12 percent of business owners today work with a coach. "Are you going to wait until it's 20, 50, 100 percent? Are you going to be in the last 20 percent to get a coach or are you going to be in the first 20 percent?" He tells me that the idea of coaching isn't new: "Every great sports team, every great sports person—they've all had a coach." And as Brad says, "A business owner is the captain of their team and they need someone to coach them from the sidelines and help them call the plays."

Entrepreneurs Need Accountability

Part of the allure of being an entrepreneur is being your own boss. So why would you want someone to coach you? Brad explains that there are three reasons why coaching works. One of them is accountability. "Business owners are by far the easiest on themselves and they let themselves get away with anything and everything." He says that even those that have very high standards know that they would achieve more if someone was watching over their shoulder every day. The second reason, Brad says, is that, "A business owner finds it hard to see the forest for the trees. As a business owner, you could probably walk into any of your friends' businesses and tell them exactly what they're doing wrong." The third reason is "The knowledge that people bring to the table. You know, our coaches bring a systemized methodology that we've used with literally more than twenty-eight thousand clients over the years." One of the major keys to closing the gap between where we are and where we want to be is accountability.

Choose a Mentor with a Great Network

Joyce Bone says mentors are critical for entrepreneurs because they share wisdom, knowledge, and experience. "They also share connections in their network and opportunity," she says. She recommends you get one or two or a small group of people that are active mentors. It can be a hands-on thing or learning through osmosis. Joyce's former boss, Raymond Cash, was her mentor. "He never sat me down and said, 'Oh, Joyce, this is the way of the world, this is what you have to do.' But I worked for him for eight years and he was a brilliant entrepreneur." Joyce watched him every day, and says she learned a tremendous amount just by being around him. "We ultimately became business partners and then he was sharing his network with me and his connections and the ability to get funds. It just opened up a whole new world for me." Joyce says if you are fortunate enough to get one or two people in your lifetime that really take an interest in you, then you are a blessed person.

Inspire Others to Want to Help You

"I have always maintained it's not what you know, it's who you know," Joyce says. "You can always hire out what you need to know but it's your ability, your emotional I.Q. really, and your ability to connect with people and get them to want to help you – that is how you're going to achieve the bigger successes in life." She says that for people to want to help you, you have to be helpful yourself. "You have to give before you get. Always look for opportunities to be of service to people that might be able to help you."

Joyce says that for over a year, she frequently extended information to the owner of a company, for opportunities that would benefit him. "And then out of the blue he's like 'Hey I have this opportunity, do you want to be a part of it?'" She says she shared information with him just because she could, and then when an opportunity came along he thought of her. "You just definitely have to give before you receive," she says.

Hot Thought

> *"Dig your well before you are thirsty."*
> – Harvey Mackay

Mentors in Your Industry

Although anyone in any industry can serve as your mentor, be sure you have some mentors who are in your chosen industry. And don't limit yourself to just those who are living. Heather Thomson considers one of her fashion mentors to be Coco Chanel. "I just think she was unbelievable, and I looked to her and I read all of her books and stories. I just think she was a powerhouse woman."

Don't limit yourself to just one mentor, when each one can help you learn something new. "My mentors came very quickly and they were all very dynamic. They each taught me something different and some still remain mentors and others not so much. But I learned invaluable lessons from Sean Combs, Jennifer Lopez, Tina and Beyonce Knowles, and Janice Combs."

Hot Seat

✓ Did anyone inspire you as a child? Did you grow up believing that you could do anything you wanted with your life?

✓ Name three people that could be your mentor or business coach? How could they help you to grow as an entrepreneur?

✓ Do you currently do anything that could inspire someone to want to help you? If not, what can you start doing now?

STAND IN THE HEAT
Chapter Nine

Biggest Mistake

"The greatest mistake you can make in life is to be continually fearing you will make one."

- Elbert Hubbard
American writer and philosopher

An extremely successful businessman and friend of mine said to me a few years ago, "Glenn, pick one thing and do it in a world class manner." Those words have been ringing in my head ever since. The biggest mistake that I have made in my professional life, by far, is not sticking to one thing. I have been easily persuaded and intrigued by "get rich quick" ideas and have typically believed the grass was greener on the other side of the fence. Perhaps you can you relate?

In my defense, I have always been willing to venture out and try something new. As a matter of fact, the last time I took the DISC personality profile, I scored ninety-nine out of one hundred in willingness to change. I am proud of that character trait, but I will have to admit that I was very ignorant in my twenties and thirties about the length of time it takes to grow a business. Having been single and very risk-tolerant for the majority of my life, I never gave my efforts time to compound. As you will learn in Chapter 14 from Brad Sugars, Founder of ActionCOACH, it takes seven years to build a solid business.

Hot Thought

> *Pick one thing and do it*
> *in a world-class manner.*

There is no shame in making mistakes. Robert Kiyosaki, author of *Rich Dad Poor Dad*, says, "In order to succeed, you *must* make mistakes. You must fail!" How do you relate to the word failure? Do you let failure affect your identity as a person or do you frame failure as a result and a learning experience? What if Thomas Edison had taken failure personally and not persisted? Well, I might be typing this page by candlelight.

What is your biggest mistake? What do you most regret in your professional life? Did you not finish that college degree? Did you not take action on an idea of your own only to see someone else capitalize? Did you trust the wrong person on your team? Did you go into a new venture with poor planning and lack of capital? Whatever your biggest mistake may be, put it in the past and get on with it!

The wake cannot drive the boat. The past is history and the future is an illusion. All we can really do is be present in the now and learn from our mistakes. Life is a cumulative experience and the ultimate score is your ability to enjoy your life on a daily basis.

Know a Little Bit About Every Aspect of Your Business

For Heather Thomson, who left a job as a celebrity stylist to launch her own shapewear brand, her biggest mistake, she says, was not having a grasp on every single aspect of her business. "You're moving so quickly but you do really have to learn to manage and be responsible for every aspect of your business, although you might be delegating some of it over." Heather says you have to learn how to delegate early on, because your business will start smaller than what it winds up being.

She once had an incident where a sales person who she thought was doing a really good job actually wasn't. Heather asked the sales person for a report as they neared the end of a year. When she looked at the report, she got that feeling of a needle scratching a record. "It was like, 'What happened? This doesn't at all look like the updates she's been giving me.'" Heather says it hit her on the head that she needed to be reported into as the president of the company. "I need one-sheeters and facts and evidence. I can't just take someone's word for it. I think you need to be your business' encyclopedia as the owner of the business with the goal being that eventually you do have all the answers."

This doesn't mean, Heather says, that you need to be an expert in every little aspect, but you should know a little bit of something about all of it, so eventually you do have all the answers. "Three years into my career there's very little now that I need to go ask someone else's advice on," she says.

The School of Entrepreneurship vs. the Ivy League

You've heard the entrepreneur success stories before. Whiz kid drops out of school to fulfill a dream and ends up making it big without the "fancy college degree." So does having a degree matter? Or can you get by on real-world business experience? It really depends on the person. "Probably the biggest mistake I made was not majoring in business in college," Mo Anderson says. Mo has had the opportunity to speak to MBA students at Yale University for four years. "I'm so intimidated by these brilliant students who learn all of these amazing things in their management program. I often wonder what I could have accomplished if I would have had that background. But you know what, I didn't have it." Mo says she had Gary Keller as her teacher, and for her, "It doesn't get any better than that."

Hire Slowly and Fire Quickly

Another mistake Mo says she made in her early days as an entrepreneur was that she should have been slow to hire and quick to fire. It something she recommends aspiring entrepreneurs pay attention to. "You see that something is not working, you need to, you just need to make a change and I would say that was, I made some mistakes in that area early on. Because, I tend to think, well, with coaching, mentoring, I can fix this. And sometimes you can't."

Wendy Reed would probably agree. "I was probably too loyal to a couple of employees in the early days and it caused some problems," she says. The employees just weren't cutting it in the management position. "They'd done really good work. I had known them for a long time so I let it slide for way too long." Looking back, Wendy wishes she would have cut each of the employees earlier, even though it would have been difficult. "Both of those times probably cost us a year or a year and a half each, which is a big price."

Brad Sugars has also learned the "Hire slow and fire quick" lesson. "A lot of people take the other way around when they hire quick and fire slow," Brad says. Put time and energy and effort up front in hiring the right person and then if they don't make it, cut your losses and move on and get another person.

Marketing Can Make or Break Your Business

Not knowing when to let go of underperforming staff can be bad for business. Another thing that can make or break your business? Marketing, Brad says. A mistake he says entrepreneurs can make is marketing too little. "There's one thing that I know about business and that is that a lack of marketing is one of businesses' biggest killers. The more marketing you can do obviously the better the growth of the business will be," he says.

Another mistake entrepreneurs make, Brad tells me, is not having a money protection system in place. Trusting people with money rather than actually having a check-up system in place with the financials is a mistake Brad says has cost him twice in his career.

New Leadership for New Stages

Looking back over the years, Dave Liniger says his single biggest mistake was not letting go of people who should have been elsewhere. "The type of person who fits a position in your organization when you have ten or twenty agents is not necessarily the same caliber of person who can help grow an international company with offices in eighty countries and one hundred thousand agents." Dave says many of his choices were not good choices. Some people worked hard but were ineffective; others just didn't have the skills necessary for the job. "The mistake you make in keeping an ineffective person on the team is everybody knows it except for the ineffective person. It's amazing."

While he has a very open relationship with his employees, and is very approachable, Dave admits that he had a tendency to avoid confrontation. "Instead of saying, 'This isn't really working for either one of us, let's separate,' I would let people hang around. It probably took me twenty years before I matured enough to understand that if you keep somebody onboard who doesn't fit any longer, you're really not doing them any favors either."

Avoiding Confrontation Hurts Everyone

Dave remembers a time when he finally had to "bite the bullet." He had four vice presidents who weren't really getting the job done. He finally got up the courage to invite each of them into his office. "We were close friends. We had been to each other's weddings and funerals. We had fought through cancers and heart attacks together and we watched our kids grow up. It was very, very difficult." Dave rehearsed what he was going to say with some trusted managers, and then told each of the vice presidents that it wasn't working out. He gave them two options: resign with a very good severance package, or be fired with two weeks' notice. "All four of them took the deal. I had hoped that we would be able to maintain a good friendship. Getting fired is like a divorce. There is a lot of emotion involved." Dave says in reality they were dead-ended.

Then Dave overheard the reaction from a couple of employees. "One of them said, 'Wow! Dave must really be bummed out. He hasn't lost an officer in the history of the company and four of them quit him on the same day!'" The most interesting comment he heard was from one of the writers in the editorial staff. He asked Dave, "What the hell did that guy have on you that you didn't fire him ten years ago?" Dave said he looked the man in the eye and told him that the former employee didn't have anything on him; that their kids grew up together and they took vacations together for twenty years. "It wasn't easy for me to let somebody like that go," Dave told him. "The difficulty of not being able to face confrontation hurts everybody."

Hot Thought

Become comfortable dealing with confrontation.

Keep Your Promises

Another big mistake that Dave says he has made in his career is promising too much and not keeping some of his promises. "We would be in meeting and somebody would say, 'Can we do this or that?' And I would say, 'Yeah, that's a good idea. We'll do that.'" But once in a meeting, someone looked right at Dave and told him that he always promises things but doesn't keep his word. Dave responded by saying that he does keep his word, but, "In reality, there were so many meetings and so many things going on that I wasn't keeping a written to-do list or minutes of the meetings. I learned that it wasn't enough just to have meetings. You needed meetings, minutes, and action times. So, it wasn't that I was promising people things with an intention of not doing them. I would promise things and forget that I'd made the promises because I was so busy doing other things."

Successful Entrepreneurship Requires Massive Energy

Scott Goodknight regrets not taking better care of his body in the past. Scott says that he used to drink a lot of alcohol. "That was part of the industry and it was accepted," he says. And for a long time there were no problems. "Near the end I think I probably drank a little too much and I think it dulled my edge." So when Scott let go of his old business in 2006, he also let go of the habit of drinking alcohol. He hasn't had a drink for almost five years now, and he also quit smoking cigarettes. "I'm just over four and a half years of no cigarettes and then I started exercising again and then I let go of drinking sodas.

"If you're going to be an entrepreneur, your body is your temple," Scott says. "You need to have tons of energy, so you need to take care of yourself. You may be listening to me and saying, 'Oh yeah that guy drank a lot of alcohol; he's an alcoholic,' or whatever. But we all have an Achilles' heel." Scott says it may not be alcohol for you, it might be pills. You might think it's okay because the pills were prescribed by a doctor. "Well, if you're using them every day to dull your pain you might want to take a look at that." Or maybe it's food, or gambling, or surfing the internet. "We've all got an Achilles' heel.

"You may think you're invincible as you're listening to this or reading this book. But you've got a weakness." Scott's advice is to get a mentor and to find out what that weakness is and keep it out in front of you. "Keep it out in front of you because it will trip you up."

Hot Thought

Identify your Achilles heel.

Trust Your Gut (It's Not About the Money)

Bob Doyle's number one mistake? "I ignored my intuition. I went against my gut," the star of *The Secret* says. "The shift came when I simply began living my passion. It wasn't about the money. Things started getting weird when I realized, 'Oh, there's all this money involved.'" Bob says he started playing "other people's games" because he saw others doing it in his industry. But that went against his rule when he first started a business, which was that he was not going to follow someone else's model just because it had been successful for them. "If it doesn't feel good to me I'm not doing it this way." That had worked extremely well for him.

"If you're going to be an entrepreneur—and I think especially when it's a small business where you're a much bigger player, you don't have a whole huge staff of employees helping you or whatever sharing your vision—you're it. You have to stay clear." Bob says as long as you keep taking action and giving value there will be financial reciprocation. "But that's the side effect, the benefit of you living fully expressed, being who you're here to be in a powerful way."

HEAT Moment

> *Bob Doyle showed Honor to his true self by putting his mission before the money — and the money showed up as a result.*

Hot Seat

✓ Are there some things you'd need to brush up on before you start your business, so that you know something about every aspect of it?

✓ Have you thought about how you might market your future business or big idea? List two ways you already have in mind.

✓ Have you had a time where you avoided confronting someone? What were the effects of avoiding the confrontation? Would you do it differently now if you had the chance?

✓ What is your Achilles' heel? Do you have a plan for keeping it from getting in your way of success?

✓ Think of a time where you went against your gut. Did it hurt you, or payoff?

STAND IN THE HEAT
Chapter Ten

Adversity into Opportunity

"Hell, there are no rules here – we're trying to accomplish something."

- Thomas A. Edison

This chapter sums up the entire purpose of this book. On the morning of February 2nd 2010, I made the *decision* to see the opportunity in my difficulty. I decided to take action and turn my adversity into opportunity. I remember getting home that night and being astonished when my search on Go Daddy revealed that StandintheHeat.com was available. To me it was a sign from God! I immediately purchased the URL and then I began planning the cover of the book, so I could sell the dream to potential interviewees. My friend, Mike McDowell, is a brilliant graphic artist and he produced a book cover that made me look like I was serious. I had my friend Derek Brooks at Brandywine Printing make a mock book that I could physically hand to someone. Taking my vision one step further, I took a picture of my book sitting on Barnes & Noble's Bestseller shelf. If you don't believe it, you will certainly never see it.

My first interview for this book was with George McKerrow, founder of LongHorn Steakhouse. In my opinion, he is one of the coolest entrepreneurs in the country and his story is the epitome of entrepreneurship. When you read about his decision during "Snow Jam 1982" in Atlanta, I am sure you will understand why I am so fond of George McKerrow. He is a master at turning adversity into opportunity!

I am friends with Steve Siebold, author of *177 Mental Toughness Secrets of the World Class*. He is the President of the National Speakers Association Million Dollar Roundtable and a seven figure earner as a non-celebrity speaker. He recently said in a video that he believes there will be more millionaires made in the next ten years than at any time in our country's history. Why? Because there are so many problems to be solved that require solutions from entrepreneurs. I like the way Steve thinks. If you want to make more money, then solve more problems for more people. It has been said that your income is in direct proportion to the value that you add to the marketplace. So, if you want to make more money simply add more value to other people's lives.

Entrepreneurs See Problems as Opportunity

George McKerrow has a great story about how he was able to turn a bad situation into a good thing! George had been trying to get a restaurant off the ground. But his partner had disappeared and money was short. He kept going, and put together a business plan. He got his dad and two other investors to back him, and they started the company back up, opening LongHorn Steaks in August of 1981.

They did a dry run and had four hundred folks attend. But the first day after they officially opened, they served just fourteen lunches and twenty-one dinners. It was downhill from there. "We were in real trouble. You start having trouble with your partners when they don't see it being successful," George says.

By January of 1982 they were in survival mode. George says he started sending employees home and was cooking, waiting on tables, and trying to figure out how to survive. But he tried to stay optimistic, and didn't give up. One day, he was sitting in the empty restaurant with a friend. They were watching TV and waiting for what they hoped would be a dinner rush. The snow started falling and it kept accumulating. He took a sign and put it in front of the restaurant with a message that said, "Drinks $1 while it snows."

"By then buses were sliding sideways, cars were stopping, and people getting out of their cars. We didn't get a whole bunch of snow, but it was really very icy. It really shut the city down. All I remember is that we rang up $700 worth of one-dollar drinks that night!" George was able to get some employees to come in, but they didn't have a full staff. He remembers that some friends got behind the bar to help out. "We just got through the night. We became the neighborhood 'cause.'" Luckily, the restaurant never lost power, and was able to stay open for the next seventy-two hours or so. "It was on a weekend, so the entire neighborhood discovered LongHorn. We were a safe haven for many people who had no power and no food."

George didn't give up when things seemed to be at their worst, and in one weekend suddenly the restaurant got tons of attention, and was also able to help people at the same time.

What will your "snowstorm" be someday when you are running your dream business?

HEAT Moment

> *George McKerrow took creative Action when he found financial opportunity in a debilitating snowstorm.*

Shift from "I Can't" to "How?"

For Joyce Bone, the adversity was like a bucket with drips of water getting dropped into it over time. Joyce says it was insult after insult in tough financial times. "I was never able to do things that I wanted to do. Drip, drip, drip and all of a sudden one day my bucket was full and it overflowed. Eventually, I hit threshold!" Joyce says she was tired of living a life of lack. "I was tired of hearing the word 'No' all the time." What she wanted was to hear the word "Yes."

"So I thought, 'Well, how am I going to hear the word yes?' Instead of saying 'I can't,' I'm going to start saying, 'How is it possible?'"

Hot Thought

> *Eliminate "I can't" from*
> *your vocabulary.*

Sick and Tired of Being Sick and Tired

Joyce says she did a paradigm shift in her brain that was triggered by a gallon of laundry detergent at Walmart. "But it wasn't really that gallon of laundry detergent. It was really a whole lifetime of not being able to do what I wanted to do; to do what my friends could do." Joyce decided that she didn't like her situation and she committed to changing it. "Not, 'Gee, that would be nice.' Not, 'I wish.' It's really the commitment that matters." She says you need to make it your foremost thought in your mind as to how you're going to make that change happen, and when you do that, you start thinking and you start getting answers. "It's some type of universal law that whatever you think about the most is what you manifest. I know that sounds kind of wacky but it's true—at least it has been in my life."

That Which You Focus Upon Grows

Joyce compares it to the Law of Attraction. "Whatever you focus on grows and whatever you ignore recedes. It's just that simple." But Joyce warns you can't just kid yourself and think, "I'll just think positive thoughts and things will happen." She says you have to take consistent action. "Whatever you are trying to accomplish, it's going to take work on your part. The world doesn't just dump things in your lap." She believes that the most successful people are the people who take the most action in life. "They're lifelong learners and they're always applying new thoughts and new strategies to their life."

Model Success to Become Successful

Scott Goodknight also believes in changing your thinking to change your life. "There's a way of looking at the world, a perception that if you look at the world in the same way that highly successful people looked at the world, then you're going to see the same opportunities." If you do this, Scott says, you will be in the same emotional state and be willing to take action like they did.

He recounts a story about Thomas Edison, where when asked about his ten thousand failures in trying to design a lightbulb, Edison supposedly said, "I didn't fail ten thousand times; I simply found ten thousand ways to successfully not create a lightbulb." The part of that story that really stuck with Scott was when Edison said, "I had to succeed because I finally ran out of things that wouldn't work."

Scott says, "I have remembered that all of these years – that if I just stick with the outcome that I want to create and I keep trying, then eventually I'm going to find something that does work."

Hot Thought

> *Reframe "failure" as "outcome."*

Create Your Dream Job

Scott had a magazine he started out of Atlanta, Georgia, called *The American Biker's Guide*. The magazine was a guide for motorcyclists telling them where to go and what to do and how to get there. Scott started expanding the magazine out in the Southeast, and went to Daytona Beach for the big bike rally and then Myrtle Beach. Folks started telling him about this guy who made a map that showed where to go and all the cool places to hang out by the beach. He tracked the guy down and used the map to get around, and says he sold twice as many ads for his magazine using the map. "I got there twice as fast as I would have by searching around on my own not knowing where to go."

Scott went back to the man and asked him about putting the map in the magazine that month. He told the man that they would print ten thousand copies. "I said, 'You'll be famous. It'll get your name out there everywhere and I'll give you credit.'" He said, "I don't think so, I'm selling these things for a buck a piece and they're eleven by seventeen, they're placemat size and that might take away from my sales." The man told Scott that he was selling one or two hundred copies. Scott offered to put an ad in the magazine for people to find the guy and buy an autographed copy of the map.

The man agreed, and during the bike week motorcycle rally, Scott noticed all these people walking around with the maps from his magazine. "I realized that they were tearing his map out and they were throwing my magazine away. It was a disaster en masse. I saw my whole business flash before my eyes. You know, like the end of your life." But then Scott says the light bulb went on. "I realized that I could make the same map that he's making and sell ads on the back instead of putting it into a magazine. I literally quadrupled the income I was making the first month I tried it." Scott decided to stop creating magazines all together: "I just created maps."

For two and a half years he went all over the country going to all of the big motorcycle rallies and selling advertising. "So I went from my original goal, which was to make about $3,000 a month and ride my motorcycle all over the country. Nobody would pay me to ride my bike all over the country and write about what I saw and did. So, I invented my own job."

Hot Thought

If your dream job doesn't exist — create it!

He says he let go of the magazine. Then the maps became so popular that people were laminating them and making them into placemats. Next he started printing them in a larger size and having them up in motorcycle shops. After that? "I said, 'Let's put them all together and we'll call it an atlas.' We called it the *Biker's Atlas.*" Scott traded his motorcycle title to a friend in exchange for money – he didn't have the money to pay to print the books. But that was only half the money he needed. He made the rest by faxing every Harley Davidson dealership in the country. "I gave them a free business listing. There were five hundred maps, there's like a thousand business listings, thousands of event listings. I literally sold out the first printout before it came off the press."

Burn Your Bridges

Scott says he had to burn all his bridges. He doesn't mean burn your networking connections or your relationships. "I didn't have the capital. I had to get in that space of 'no matter what.' I burned all bridges and then my subconscious mind start kicking out the ideas of how to make it happen." Scott compares says it's like that line "necessity is the mother of invention." It has to be a must. "So many entrepreneurs say, 'I want to open a business. I want to make more money.' It won't happen. It has to be a must. And you can't just have a plan. You've got to put everything on the line.

"Volunteer yourself to catch the American spirit of being an entrepreneur and just don't give up no matter what. It's going to be hard. That's what you should take pride in."

Hot Seat

✓ Think of a time you were able to turn a problem into an opportunity. Hasn't happened to you yet? Think of some problems that you could have when you start your own business. Can any of those be turned into opportunities?

✓ What are three things that you think you "can't" do?

✓ What are you tired of in your life? Can you commit to changing it?

✓ What is your goal or plan? Think of a way that you could "burn all your bridges" to get there.

STAND IN THE HEAT
Chapter Eleven

Proudest Accomplishment

"You are never given a dream without also being given the power to make it true. You may have to work at it, however."

**- Richard Bach
American writer**

Without a doubt, my proudest accomplishment has been becoming a father. It has motivated me to get off my butt and write this book. For the first forty years of my life, I never took on too much responsibility and I openly admit to having been commitment phobic in my personal and professional life. Fortunately, there is hope for we late bloomers!

One look at my resume validates that I never liked to stay in one place too long. From a business standpoint, however, finishing this book has been the proudest accomplishment of my life. I have been an avid reader since graduating college and I have amassed a rather impressive personal library. I have always been inspired by people who have the fortitude and willingness to share their failures and successes in a book. I had always dreamed of writing a book of my own, but thought that writing a book was an ultra marathon reserved for other people – not me.

What is your proudest accomplishment? Is it a personal or business victory? Do you have a proudest accomplishment yet? If not, that's okay. The fact that you are reading this book suggests that you are searching and your victory is on its way. Keep dreaming, keep searching, and never give up. I have always believed there is truth in Richard Bach's quote. You wouldn't be dreaming about whatever you hope to do if you didn't also possess the power to make that dream a reality.

I don't dream of being a world-renowned chef, the leader of the free world, or a stay-at-home dad. I dream what I dream because I know that I am supposed to become what I dream about. My dream is to inspire people to realize their greatest potential through my books and speeches. If the wisdom from these great entrepreneurs can somehow move you closer to realizing your greatest accomplishment, then I will be completely honored!

Happiness is a Choice

When they look back, some of our entrepreneurs are most proud of their professional accomplishments. Others are most proud of their family. What will you be most proud of when you look back on your journey? It may depend on where you are in your life when someone like me asks you!

What is Herman Cain most proud of? "I've been married to the same woman for forty-two years and she's been married to me for forty-two years," he says. He's also proud of the job he and his wife did in raising their two kids, who have many of the values they share. Both children are married with kids of their own, and Herman says they're both self-supporting. "They're not looking for a handout and not looking for the government to do it for them, and they also realize there's no department of happy in Washington, D.C. You have to create your own department of happy!" Herman believes if you want something, you go out and work for it.

Hot Thought

> *Create your own*
> *"Department of Happy."*

Fight for Your Life

While Heather says she's really most proud of her children, marriage, and friendships, she says in regards to her business she is most proud of the fight – the perseverance – that it took to get to where she is now. "We came up with an original idea. I hold four patents on the original Yummie Tummie Tank." It's fun, Heather tells me, because her kids can someday say, "Mommy was an inventor."

Heather started her business at the beginning of 2008. Three months in, Oprah Winfrey found her and put the tank on the "favorite things" show. The knockoffs came out of the woodwork after she launched her product. "You couldn't believe how many people copied my idea, and it was right when I was starting my business. They ranged from the mass market to the high end. I mean, everybody knocked off the three panel system. And I was only patent pending at the time and that has been the greatest challenge really of my business.

"So when the patents filed we let people know that we indeed owned the idea. Some people backed off and some people came on stronger. I got sued. That drained my company every day of money, emotion . . . Now, when you get a $390,000 bill from your lawyer it does a hell of a lot to your cash flow."

Teamwork Makes the Dream Work

While some entrepreneurs might be proud in telling people they did something all on their own, for George McKerrow, it's quite the opposite. "The thing I'm most proud of is that LongHorn's success is not my personal success. I didn't do it alone. I did it with a lot of great people who did a ton of the work." George says he inspired the team and guided them in any way that he could.

These days, he loves meeting people who tell him, "My dad took me to LongHorn." "I met my wife at LongHorn." "I still work at LongHorn and you hired me twenty years ago." But back then, he says, giving someone a good job, a good lifestyle, and making them feel secure was the hardest thing he ever did. "I remember hiring the first manager at LongHorn saying, 'My biggest fear isn't that you're going to like this job or that you can do the job. My biggest fear is that I'm taking on the responsibility of telling you that your paycheck's going to be good every two weeks.' That's a big responsibility."

Today, George says he and business partner Ted Turner employ three thousand people at Ted's Montana Grill, and don't outsource any jobs. "We give people of all ages an opportunity to work. Whether they're in college and need a part-time job, a single parent that needs a full-time job, or a career-oriented person who wants to get into a management job. That's more than I can say for a lot of big companies today."

Culture is Key

Wendy Reed is also a proud mom. "I'm most proud of my children because they're just remarkable," she says. But in business, Wendy is really proud of how she and her colleagues grew InfoMentis, the company she founded, which is now part of The TAS Group. "The culture of the company just continues to come back to us from customers and employees – even people that left here because they weren't maybe cutting it." Wendy says she recently met with a woman that worked at the company eight or nine years ago. The woman was a very good person and could do some things well but just wasn't a good fit for the company. "She just was at breakfast with me saying, 'Out of all the jobs I ever had, this was my absolute favorite one,' even though she didn't work out. The culture that we have created here is what I'm probably the most proud of."

125

STAND IN THE HEAT

Contribution

Scott Goodknight says he's done many things to be proud of, including serving our country and being a Ranger. But he is most proud of the community that he has built in Atlanta with his Mental M.A.P.S. program. Mental M.A.P.S. is designed to help people take back control of their internal "GPS" and program themselves with new "maps" or belief systems. Scott says every week men and women get together to support each other. From authors, to business owners, to budding restaurateurs, the group is very diverse.

"We have some very foundational rules about not judging and not giving advice. We're just there to hold the space and support each other and encourage each other, and to be accountable men and women taking action every single day. We meet once a week but everybody is checking in with each other every single day." Scott says he is most proud of the men and women of the Mental M.A.P.S. community; they are like family to him.

And of course, Scott says, "I'm proud of being an entrepreneur."

Hot Seat

✓ Do you agree with Herman Cain that "Happiness is a choice"? What are three things that make you happy?

✓ What are you most proud of right now? What will you be most proud of five years from now? Ten years from now?

✓ How will having a team help you to be successful in your future entrepreneurial venture? Or do you think you'll be "going it alone"?

✓ What kind of culture do you see your business having someday? Do you think that years after they're gone former employees will still say good things about your company?

STAND IN THE HEAT
Chapter Twelve

Advice for the Struggling Entrepreneur

"Where there is no struggle, there is no strength."

- Oprah Winfrey

My best advice for any entrepreneur who is struggling in the direction of his or her dream is twofold: stay connected to your passion and learn patience. I strongly believe that passion is the key to having everything you want in your life. Think about a time in your life when you wanted something so badly that you could taste it! Was it a new car, home, college degree, or winning the affection of a significant other? When we are totally passionate and committed to an end result of any kind, we usually get what we want. Wouldn't you agree?

Have you ever met someone who you felt was less talented than you, but they were more "successful" than you? Odds are they had a level of passion about their endeavor that consumed them at all hours of the day. If you truly love what you do, your vocation will become your vacation. What can you do better than the largest number of people in the world? What can you do in an extraordinary fashion that most people fear? Determine what you would do for free because you are so passionate about it and figure out how to get paid. Find your sweet spot and constantly fuel your passion!

My second piece of advice is to constantly grow your patience. Admittedly, I have failed rather miserably at being patient. As a result, I have jumped ship too quickly on numerous occasions in my career. You must give your efforts time to compound. If patience were a class in school, then I would have probably earned an F. Invariably it takes more time and money to get any venture off the ground than originally planned. Whether it is your venture or you are along for the ride, expect a bumpy road.

It has been my experience that things rarely happen on my projected timeframe. Regardless of having an airtight business plan and an epic level of passion, events can occur that are beyond our control. As an entrepreneur, you must have the confidence, determination, and vision to venture out on your own in the first place. Most entrepreneurs, however, need to learn to dance with the duality that exists between ambition and patience.

It goes without saying that entrepreneurs have to be leaders and leadership can be stressful. Entrepreneurs must first lead themselves before they can effectively lead others. We must win the battles that rage in our mind on a daily basis.

A lot of my stress lies in my expectations around timeframes. In our world of instant gratification, I want everything to develop yesterday and I get very frustrated when I can't seem to make things happen faster. One of my favorite quotes of all time is from Tony Robbins. He says, "Frustration precedes breakthrough." If that is the case, then I feel that I am about to have a breakthrough that rivals the Big Bang! Perturbation is defined as a "Cause of mental disquiet, disturbance, or agitation." I get perturbed when I feel like I am not doing enough quickly enough, but then I have to remind myself that without pressure and time, a lump of coal would never turn into a diamond. I constantly say to myself, "Be patient, Grasshopper."

Hot Thought

> *"Frustration precedes breakthrough."*
> *— Tony Robbins*

The struggles that entrepreneurs face can be plentiful and painful. They can come in the form of limited working capital, not enough hours in the day, wearing too many hats, branding, hiring competent staff, having efficient systems, or even working for someone else while we pursue our dream. If our "Why" is big enough, however, the struggle will always be worthwhile. My advice is to never, ever, ever lose sight of your dream or lose your passion!

Adversity Makes Us Stronger

It's like that old saying, Heather Thompson says, "'Whatever doesn't kill you makes you stronger.' You just learn so much in life, and you might change directions. What you initially set out to do as an entrepreneur may not be what you ultimately wind up doing," she says.

But if you want to run your own business and you want to do your own thing, "Don't ever stop. Get there." Heather says that history is a sort of training for the future. "You have to take your hits and you have to learn from them, and like my kids' godfather Dirk always says to me, 'It's not how you hit the mat, it's how you get back up.'"

Someday you're going to read this chapter again, and I think, and Heather would agree, that it can't be said enough how important it is that you take the challenges on headfirst and keep moving forward. Why? "You keep on going because adversity makes you stronger."

Accountability

"I believe the reason most entrepreneurs fail is because they don't have accountability," Mo Anderson tells me. Is she right? Picture yourself in your current job. If your boss and their boss and their boss and beyond, all disappeared, would you still be able to achieve the goals that had been set? Complete the workload needed to achieve those goals? In a reasonable time? Maybe not. You might take a few extra days off, maybe hit the golf course or go to the mall. Sometimes it can be hard to focus when you don't have a leader or a "boss."

Mo recommends that struggling entrepreneurs is to get a coach or mentor who can help them evaluate the business model. "Many times entrepreneurs struggle because they don't have a business model. They're just flying by the seat of their pants. And having a coach who can guide you to tweak the business model or improve the business model or evaluate it is critically important." That coach or mentor needs to be someone that you can go to any time, maybe even on a weekly basis, so that they can hold you accountable for the things you need to do to achieve your goals. You're still the "boss of you," only now, you have someone extra in your cheering section when you succeed. And when you don't that person is there to help keep you going.

Associate with Great Thinkers

"You are what you eat." Maybe. But in entrepreneurship, it's more like "You are who you're around." What?

Trish McCarty says "We are an average of the five people that we put around us. It can even be people in your head." One of Trish's five? Benjamin Franklin. "He's not real; I talk to him all day long. I go, 'Benjamin, what would you tell me to do in this particular place?'" Trish says this will influence you more than anything. "The five people who are in your head the most are going to influence your thinking the most. So you're gonna be an average of those five people."

Hot Thought

> *If you don't program your mind, someone else will.*

This means, Trish says, that you need to be very, very careful about the five people that are influencing you. When selecting those five people, make sure that they believe in you and if you don't have five people that believe in you, Trish says to make them up! "Make them be the Queen of England and Jesus, or whomever you want in your head to talk to you and tell you how great you are and that you're on the right track, and then just keep going. Somebody is going to program your brain; it might as well be you!"Better start thinking of your five before I steal some of the good imaginary ones!

Grasp Reality

Okay, now we go from talking in our heads to Benjamin Franklin, to an entrepreneur who says that struggling entrepreneurs have to be willing to accept reality. "Reality dictates that sometimes you have to let go to succeed," says George McKerrow. If you find yourself in a place where you just can't make something work, you have to cut your losses. It's okay to start over." But at the same time, George says you have to have foresight and the ability to plan. While foresight can be learned, George believes it's the way you're wired that helps give you that ability. "They react to events around them and they react to what's happened to them in the past. They make judgments going forward based on lots of things that are either happening now or in the past."

Make the Journey

George says he makes most of his judgments based on what he wants the future to be and what he sees as realistic down the road. Once you set that course in the future, you can make a plan to get there step by step. "Life is a journey, not a destination." George believes that there are a lot of people out there who want to just end up at the destination, and skip the journey it would take to get there. "There's a whole generation of lost people out there who are living on the sideline. My biggest fear for my thirty-something-year-old daughter is that we taught our children to be destination-oriented instead of journey-oriented."

Society has changed the way we do things, George tells me. "When I played sports as a kid, I got cut if I wasn't good enough. If I was the best player in that position, I got to play. If not, I sat on the bench. Over the last thirty years, that's all changed." If you're a parent, you may see this happen with your son or daughter's teams or activities: "Everybody plays, everybody bats, everybody gets a trophy, and everybody gets an ice cream sundae. That's not how real life works."

Focus on Your Core Offering

Another thing to avoid if you're a struggling entrepreneur? Trying to do too many things at once. George says it's one downfall of being a successful entrepreneur. "There were several dreams I had at LongHorn that we folded. At one point, we got too diversified at LongHorn. I met with everybody and said, 'All we're going to do is worry about how we cut and cook steaks. Because it's LongHorn Steaks.'"

Expand When Everything is Cheap

An entrepreneur should always be paying close attention to what the economy is doing to help keep their business positioned properly. In a down economy, says Brad Sugars, 20 to 30 percent of your competitors will be eliminated. "People are always looking to do better business in down economies so they're looking for more values. When it's a booming economy most customers aren't looking to do other business. They're just looking to do the business that they've got, but people are looking for new places to buy from. They're looking for better value so everything is cheaper. There's no better time to expand than when everything's cheap and when people are looking for new places to do business."

Brad says the negative economies last for a period of one to two years before they start to turn around, and it generally takes most in the marketplace four to five years before they recognize the economy has turned around. So if you're paying attention, you'll be aware of a shift before most of your competition.

Sacrifice

If you're someone who is still working to earn a paycheck, but wants to be "free," remember that it's good to have income coming in from that j-o-b while building something on the side, Joyce Bone says. "It's going to take a tremendous amount of energy from the person who already has a full-time job, but has the dream and the desire to start their own venture." Joyce says you have to start small and start building your future business on your own time. That may mean that you have to get up early before you go to work or stay up late after you get home from work. "You're gonna be tired and you're just gonna have to say, 'Okay, I'm willing to be tired in order to create the lifestyle, the dream, the goal that I have for myself and for my family.'" Are you willing to sacrifice sleep, watching TV, Saturdays and Sundays, and vacation? You have to be willing to so that you can invest that time into your dream.

"It's not easy to do it that way but it's not impossible." Joyce made sacrifices when she use what little time she could gather up to write the book *Millionaire Moms: The Art of Raising a Business and a Family at the Same Time*. "I was already tapped out. I've got three kids. I was running Millionaire Moms and I had a full plate. I was going to MBA school. I was doing all kinds of crazy stuff and all of a sudden I was writing this book." Joyce says she got up at five in the morning at least three times a week for seven months and wrote the book at five in the morning. "Did I like getting up and doing that? No. But I did it because I was committed to writing the book. Because I wanted to help other people succeed, so you do what you need to do."

Joyce says that if you're really and honestly committed to make something happen you have to make a covenant with

STAND IN THE HEAT

yourself. "You have to be willing to do whatever it takes to make your dream a reality." But taking care of yourself can be part of it too. "If you're overweight and you're working full-time you're not gonna have the energy required to do that thing that you want to do for yourself, [to] create your own financial freedom." So you have to get your lifestyle choices in line, she tells me. Start exercising, eating better foods—whatever you can to support yourself physically and mentally. "It's not easy and that's why most people don't do it. It takes a lot of energy and, yes, like I said commitment. You've got to be committed and be persistent."

Live Your Vision Your Way

"Initially, I labored under the impression that to be an entrepreneur the way I wanted to, I had to do it all myself," says Bob Doyle. "It wasn't until I really learned to accept coaching in various forms that I really got the full, rich experience of being an entrepreneur."

While Bob always wants his business to be successful and to bring in revenue, he doesn't have a vision that includes employees and big buildings. "I love the model that I have. I get to work from home. I touch, you know, potentially millions of people because I work online. I don't have to deal with the headaches of employees and things like that."

For the parts of his business that he doesn't enjoy, Bob says, he finds people who like doing those things and he outsources to them. It's just a model that works great for people like me." Bob loves that he gets to be the CEO of a company and work in his pajamas if he wants to, and make videos and talk to people.

"I can be wearing sweatpants from the waist down and a shirt and no one has to be the wiser, right?" *Sure Bob, I won't tell anyone you sometimes work in your PJs!*

Believe You Deserve Success

"As long as I communicate my message and contribute value that's the job of an entrepreneur, to make sure that their company or their project or whatever is contributing maximum value while staying in the state of passion about what they're doing. That's success," Bob says. So if you're adding value and acting in a spirit of service, how can you not make money? "I will tell you how," Bob says, "If you don't believe you deserve it! There are plenty of people who deliver considerable value, but don't believe they deserve financial success and therefore suffer." But don't forget, even if you believe, it will still take work, even if you sometimes work in sweats. "There was a lot of action, a lot of learning. But I enjoyed every minute of it because I was getting value from the process. I enjoyed learning about marketing. I enjoyed learning what kind of sales page works. It was like a puzzle."

Lisa Levison also says you have to believe. "By believing that you're an entrepreneur and believing that you've got something; that makes you strong enough to get out there and do it." Lisa says you can't lose sight of what it takes to get there. Start with something that you know how to do, something you can get a following for, she says. And keep it simple. "Whatever your crazy idea is – start with something that you can control, master, and see from beginning to end." Lisa says oftentimes people believe that, "I can sell it if I can think of it," but Lisa says you have to get in there and understand how to sell it; understand how it works. "Keep it simple and build on the smaller concept and make it bigger, bigger, bigger. One step at a time. But no idea is too crazy."

Stress is Information

Stress. It's the reason Dr. Kathleen Hall has seen women leave things they love. "Whether it's financial stress; whether their marriage is struggling because of their career; whatever the situation that they've come up against, they haven't learned the resilience. Especially women because we do experience stress differently than men; we experience more of it and it has a quicker affect on our physical and our psychological systems." Every entrepreneur, whether a man or woman needs to learn stress management techniques, Dr. Hall says. "Don't run away from stress. I think stress provides a lot of information. You need to look at your stressors and your triggers and because it's a lot of information about you." She says that stress is not bad, it's simply informational; it can tell you a lot about yourself. It might make you realize something, such as telling you what direction you should go in; or which direction you shouldn't go in. "Stress has a lot of question marks after it, not an exclamation point. And I look at stress as an invitation."

Dr. Hall says she has dealt with so many "successful" people. They may look successful, anyway. "When I ask them about the three most important things in their life a lot of them will almost cry and say 'That was my wife,' 'It was my children,' 'It was when I had that little farm but I sold it for my penthouse.'" Dr. Hall says that too often, we forget the core of who we are. Success in your world should be being happy, being fulfilled, and having wonderful rich life that you love. "The biggest gift you can give your family, spouse and company is the gift of stress resilience."

Hot Thought

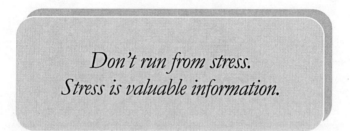

*Don't run from stress.
Stress is valuable information.*

Stop and Reflect

Sometimes, you should just pause. When you feel like you are struggling to "make it" or to go out on your own, here is what Herman Cain says you should do: "Stop, take a deep breath, and reflect on where you are, where you're trying to get to, and what you might need to do different in order to get there. It might be time to reset and re-plan.

But you gotta first stop, take a deep breath, sit back and evaluate where you are, what your resources are – and then go from there.

Hot Seat

✓ What adversity are you willing to go up against to achieve your goals?

✓ Who can keep you accountable? Do you have someone to be your "boss" once you're on your own?

✓ Who are the five people you want around you to influence you? Are any of them only in your head?

✓ What sacrifices are you willing to make? List three things you would give up or change in your life to put more time towards your goals.

✓ Think of an incident recently that stressed you out. Looking back, what information should you have learned from that stress?

Section III

Take Massive Action

"Action! And this time believe!"

A mentor of mine used to say, "When in doubt, take action!" A mediocre plan violently executed is better than a perfect plan that is never acted upon. When I began writing this book, I swung for the fence. I reached out to some really big named entrepreneurs and asked for interviews. As a consequence, I got some really big "No's." Oh well, nothing ventured nothing gained. Perhaps I will revisit those folks again when I write my second book?

When you are passionately pursuing your purpose in life, it is obvious to others. Your enthusiasm, conviction, and intention shine like a neon sign and are infectious. I have always believed that it is imperative to take action in our fleeting moments of inspiration. I say fleeting moments because those little voices that can creep into our thinking and keep us in fear are never too far away.

It's not what we know that changes our lives, but what we *do*. I will ask you a question that I have asked thousands of people all over the world. What are the two things that we must do to get in better shape physically? Anywhere on the planet I get the correct answer in less than two seconds – exercise and eat right. If the solution is so simple, then why is seventy percent of the population overweight? The answer lies in the fact that there is a great divide the size of the Grand Canyon between knowing and doing!

I will be the first to admit that I have always struggled with discipline and focus. I will define discipline as the willingness to do the things you need to do even when you don't feel like doing them. For most people it is easier to live life based on our desires in the moment rather than from our commitments. Have you ever struggled with discipline or is it just me?

Hot Thought

*It's not what we know that
changes our lives, it's what we do.*

The great thing about taking massive action is that there is a symbiotic loop between action and emotion. Motion creates emotion and when we feel good we do good. Action tends to positively affect our emotions and when our emotions are positive we tend to take more action. I have always been one to make my bed the moment my feet hit the floor in the morning. It is a simple action that gives me a feeling of accomplishment at the very beginning of the day. The same principle is exercised by professional golfers on the putting green. They usually warm up with eighteen-inch putts as opposed to three-foot putts. Effective action breeds positive feelings and positive feelings breed more effective action.

STAND IN THE HEAT
Chapter Thirteen

First Entrepreneurial Venture

"A mind that is stretched by a new experience can never go back to its old dimensions."

**- Oliver Wendell Holmes Jr.
Associate Justice, Supreme Court**

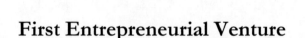

I first realized that I had the entrepreneurial spirit at age ten when I went door to door in our neighborhood selling raffle tickets to raise money for my little league football team. The grand prize for the kid who sold the most tickets was a really cool jacket and I had to have it. It was my first "brass ring."

I remember striking out on my own on the weekends and staying out all day selling tickets in pursuit of that coveted jacket. We didn't go out in teams. I went about it alone. I do recall some rejection, but mostly I recall the purpose that drove me to succeed. I had never taken a class or read a book on entrepreneurship or sales. I believe it was instinct.

I remember like it was yesterday knocking on the door of a home that had a "No Soliciting" sign displayed. Although I didn't know the definition of the word "soliciting" at ten years old, I did understand the definition of the word "no." My head was telling me to pass on this house, but my heart was set on winning that jacket! So, I rang the doorbell.

When the lady of the house answered the door, she pointed at the sign and said with a scowl, "Don't you know what 'No Soliciting' means?" In my gut I knew what the sign meant, but since I didn't technically know the definition of "soliciting," I made my cutest little boy face and said "No." After I stated my case, she bought a ticket!

It was at that woman's door that I first learned the magic of being bold. I had already learned that lesson on the football field, but now I had learned it in the world of commerce. Entrepreneurs have to be bold and have to be able to handle rejection and take arrows in the back. Whether or not your first venture is a success, celebrate the fact that you took a chance, assumed risk and broke through your fear.

Competing with the Boys

Heather Thompson's first try at becoming an entrepreneur was when she was about thirteen years old. She decided to start her own lawn mowing business. "I saw all the guys on my block earning money by mowing the neighbors' lawns and I thought, 'Well my dad's got a lawnmower, and I've got two arms and two legs, so why can't I earn some money?'" But it was a shock, she says, when people wouldn't give her the job because she was a girl. "I was born in 1970, so we were certainly in an era of change." But luckily for Heather, some of the guys she played tackle football with felt bad that she couldn't earn any money, so they made her a part of their group. "They would give me a couple of their jobs and give me half the money, and that wasn't good enough for me." Heather said she kept pounding the pavement until she had about four lawn mowing jobs.

"I guess I always had that drive in me," she says. "But I don't think I really realized I was an entrepreneur until I actually started Yummie Tummie."

Youngsters Need Executive Skills Too

Trish McCarty says that during her time in corporate America, she wondered why kids weren't being taught certain skills. She was hired out of college by AT&T. "At the time AT&T and companies like IBM really took a lot of pride in having the best executives. They hired me to become a woman executive, because at the time they didn't have enough females, so they had this system that I literally fell into to bring a young woman up into this executive power role really quickly." Trish says that sometimes meant two to three days of training out of a five day period. She says she used to think, "Why don't we teach kindergarteners how to shake hands, have executive protocol, and become a world ambassador? Why aren't basic executive skills being taught to our youngest people?" Now, in her StarShine Academy, Trish says a lot of the things they do with the kids today is directly related to that training.

She credits that training with helping her to be successful, but also says that she was born with the entrepreneurial spirit. Both her parents, as well as her siblings, had their own companies or business ventures. Trish herself started a dinosaur club in the second grade. She says the club was for people who really liked dinosaurs and wanted to draw them. "I used to draw these dinosaurs and I used to sell them. It was hilarious. I mean, kids would buy them with their lunch money." But she didn't stop looking for ways to make money when grade school was over. In college, she sold her notes to people who didn't take their own; she sold paintings, and sold macramé hangers for pots and plants. "Even when I was in corporate America I always had something going on the side. I've always liked money."

Entrepreneurship and Your DNA

George McKerrow decided in the eighth grade that he wanted to be an entrepreneur. He says that was when he learned how to spell the word "entrepreneur." "I'll never forget when I told my eighth grade Civics teacher that I wanted to be an entrepreneur or President of the United States. He said, 'George, there's no chance you're going to be president of the United States.' So, here I am. I had a dream."

In high school, George says he made and sold potholders, mass producing hundreds of them and selling them door to door. He also had a paper route. "That's an entrepreneur venture. If you don't collect correctly, you never get paid! If you under collect, you don't get paid." For gas money, George worked in the restaurant business. After school, he got a job as a bartender, and later operated a small restaurant in the mountains of West Virginia.

"There are people who are cut out to be entrepreneurs and there are people who are not," George says. He believes his independent spirit is in his DNA. "I think it's in your character. There are characteristics about those of us who are entrepreneurial that are different than those who are not. I've watched people who aren't cut out to be entrepreneurs try really hard and still fail."

Partners and Money

By 1980, George had decided he was ready to open his own restaurant. He and a friend, Hugh Connerty decided to build LongHorn Steaks on Peachtree Road in Atlanta. George took a bartending job, working by night to pay the bills, and working by day to build the restaurant. Then came a roadblock. "We got halfway through the process and I realized that Hugh didn't have the money. A lot of people would have just walked away. I guess that's one thing I'm pretty proud of. I felt like I could finish it, so I did." George says that to him, the true freedom of life is being able to have choices. "I really wanted to control my own destiny."

Working for Other People

As a kid Brad Sugars used to sell his Christmas presents to his brothers. It would have been a pretty safe bet back in those days to say that Brad would grow into an entrepreneur.

Hot Thought

> *It may be an advantage if you aren't good at working for other people.*

Eventually he wanted to control his destiny, by being his own boss. "I learned pretty early on that I wasn't good at working for other people. I think that was a pretty obvious thing. After you've done a few different businesses or you've looked at a few different things, and you started building stuff on your own and had some success, I think you kind of realize, 'This is what I'm naturally meant to do.'" Brad says that too many people go on for too long working in a job even when they know they should be working for themselves. "Once you realize that you should be working for yourself, the best thing you can do is acknowledge that realization and promptly do it."

What's Your Unique Selling Proposition?

Joyce Bone had her first business at five years old! What did she do at that young age? Sell frogs, of course. "I found an area where we lived where there this frog explosion. There was like all these little frogs just hopping around, so I got a shoebox and I scooped up a bunch of them, and then I went door to door and I sold them to the neighbors – a quarter for the big ones and a dime for the little ones. And even at that young age, Joyce knew that she needed a way to make her product stand out from the competition. "My unique selling proposition was that frogs are very good for your garden and they help control bugs. You want to have frogs on your property, so that you don't have a lot of bugs." Selling frogs wasn't an easy business, but Joyce wanted to do something different. "I had a lot of competition with the lemonade stands because there were a lot of kids in the neighborhood. I wanted something unique."

If You Don't Ask, the Answer is Always "No"

Like Heather Thompson and many others, Scott Goodknight saw an opportunity to make money by mowing lawns as a kid. "I realized very quickly that I could make more money in a couple of hours than my friends who worked eight hours a day in the local Dairy Queen, Kentucky Fried Chicken, or McDonald's for five or six bucks an hour."

But it was after his time in the Army that Scott really found his entrepreneurial side. He was working at Gold's Gym, and created an events calendar, and went around to business in the shopping center the gym was in selling advertisements. Scott says he made several hundred dollars, and printed the calendars on the printer at work. "We set them on the counter there and I don't know how useful it was, but I remember the feeling of how easy it was to go out and make a couple hundred dollars. Then, it just came in every month!" Scott says that the businesses were glad to be included in the calendar, and were happy to pay the twenty-five dollars. "That's when I first realized, 'Hey I can make money really fast.'" The money Scott made from selling gym memberships wasn't much. "It was maybe thirty-five dollars and it was a pretty big ordeal to get somebody to sign up and commit to two years to join the gym. So I started really realizing that I could do something with my ability to create value, solve a problem, and ask people for the sale."

Hot Thought

*Have the courage to ask
for what you want.*

The key, Scott tells me, is that there's got to be a problem, and you've got to have a unique solution. But, you also have to have the courage to ask for it. Scott has an old saying, he's not sure who gave it to him; he might have even made it up on his own after years of sales training – "If you don't ask, the answer is always 'No.'" Scott says, "If you don't ask, there's no way that anybody can tell you yes. So just get over the fear of asking and somebody is going to say 'Yes.'"

Entrepreneurial Spirit

Dr. Kathleen Hall came from a long line of entrepreneurs. From the time she was two years old she was influenced by her grandfather and her father. Her father was a cracker and cookie salesman for National Biscuit Company. He was inspired by motivational speaker Glenn Turner, and Kathleen would hear her father listening to Glenn Turner's tapes. "I went to sleep every night of my life with Glenn Turner, *Dare to be Great*. And my father, he would look at us and he'd look at me especially and he'd go, 'Don't ever forget: dare to be great.'"

She was about eight years old when she started collecting cans and things left over from dinner. She'd clean them out, price them, and make her own grocery store in an empty space under the stairs. "I made play money and I would make the other kids in my family come and shop there and get the money." By the time Kathleen was ten she had her own potholder business, she'd sell them on weekends to the neighbors for a quarter, and do special orders for holidays. By twelve she was babysitting, then at fifteen years old she had a beauty salon in her garage, with a little help from her father. "I got him to loan me money to buy a beauty chair and I started doing all the women in the neighborhood's hair."

Her first "proper job" she says came at sixteen, working for J. C. Penney. "I worked in the gift wrapping department and I think I made fifty cents an hour." Then she became a wig expert, and quadrupled their sales on wigs because she would wear the wigs herself to show them off. "I'd grab people as they were walking by and I'd go, 'Haven't you always wanted to be a blond?' And of course they'd go, 'Oh sure.' I had the entrepreneurial spirit even though I was working for a big company." Kathleen says you don't have to own only a small corporation to have fun and have an entrepreneur's attitude. "You cannot take someone's soul. You have to learn how to nourish that soul because it will work with you and for you in a corporation and grow it. So if they would look instead, look at the spark that's in everybody and listen instead of telling. Listen more."

Profits vs. Wages

Dave Liniger's first entrepreneurial venture was deciding at sixteen that he wanted to make a million dollars in the real estate business. He had read a few books that influenced him, including *How I Turned $1,000 into a Million in Real Estate – in My Spare Time*, by William Nickerson. Liniger says that William Nickerson was a postman in Southern California back in the early 1950s. He found a house while on his postal route that he bought, fixed up, and sold for a profit. Then he kept doing it until he had a very large empire of rental properties.

By the age of nineteen, Dave was in the military in Tucson, Arizona. "It was there that I bought my first fix-up property," he says. "That property cost about $10,000. I sold it for a $5,000 profit about a year later. That was interesting to me, because I was making $99 a month in the Air Force as an airman." He had three part-time jobs: delivering newspapers to 7-Eleven's and a newspaper route, working at a filling station at night, and a movie theater on weekends. "Between those four jobs, which I worked seventeen hours a day, I was making $400. Compare the $400 a month working those hours to a $5,000 profit on the one property I bought." Dave was hooked.

Hot Thought

> *Wages are for employees.*
> *Profits are for entrepreneurs.*

He decided to become a real estate investor. "I never had any intention of being a real estate agent because I didn't feel like I could sell. And to be quite honest with you, at nineteen years old I looked like I was ten years old." He went to a local company and got his real estate license, with the intention of saving the commission on the properties he was buying and fixing up. "After about six months, I noticed that there was a bunch of old people in that company. Some of them are forty or fifty years old. I was twenty years old and thinking 'Wow!' I thought if they could make some sales, maybe I could too." Dave struggled for a long time, but says he found the right trainer and the right mentor, and eventually, he became a success. Later he got his residency and broker's license and then started his own company.

A Dog-Eat-Dog World

Sometimes entrepreneurs decide to strike out on their own because they're in search of a challenge. That was the case for Herman Cain. He first realized that he wanted to make a career change after his first few years working for the Department of the Navy as a mathematician. "I realized I was working at a very secure, very predictable environment. I could have stayed with the government as a civil servant for twenty-five or thirty years, retired, got my retirement going and done something else." But he started to feel dissatisfied in that environment. He didn't want predictability.

HEAT Moment

Herman Cain showed great Enthusiasm when he left the security of his government job for a new world of opportunities in corporate America

"I wanted challenge. I wanted to go beyond what I ever thought I'd ever be able to do, and that's when I got the inkling that I wanted to get into the corporate world. I knew that in corporate America there's a lot more risks associated with just a normal job than it is in the government, civil service environment. And I wasn't afraid of that risk." Herman says when he would tell friends that he was thinking of going to work in the private sector, they'd ask him why he'd want to leave the security of his government job.

"They said, 'You're going to leave all of this? You've got thirty days of vacation here, four weeks of vacation.' 'You're going to leave that? You're going to go in that dog-eat-dog world of corporate America?' I said, 'It's the dog-eat-dog part that makes me want to join it.'"

Hot Seat

✓ Have you already had your first venture into the world of entrepreneurship? What was it? What did you learn about yourself in the process?

✓ Are there skills you learned early on in life that you believe will make you a successful entrepreneur now?

✓ Do you have a unique selling proposition for your future venture?

✓ Do you look forward to the challenge of making a major career change? Or is that what's holding you back?

STAND IN THE HEAT
Chapter Fourteen

Start-up Phase

"Whatever you're thinking, think bigger!"

- Tony Hsieh
Co-Founder, Zappos

I have always been enticed and intrigued by the possibilities of a start-up. Like a new relationship, there is wonder and excitement surrounding a new idea that has the potential to become something great. However, the odds of a new business making it to the ten-year mark are slim to none.

Eighty percent of new businesses fail within the first five years. Of those businesses that survive, eighty percent fail with the next five years. It would be a great understatement to say that starting a new business venture can be fraught with dangerous waters.

I have been involved in a number of start-ups in my business career, but the one that held the most promise and excitement was in the height of the dot-com era. I was a co-founder of a dot-com company that was positioned in the Kindergarten through grade twelve market and had the intention of creating tutorials for students after school. We had a very alluring story and a very high-profile Chairman of the Board with an internationally recognized name. We had the attention of the president of a major motion picture production company who was interested in providing state-of-the-art technology for the tutorials. We had an expensive business plan that had been massaged and anointed by a best-of-breed consulting firm. We had a public shell that allowed us to do a reverse merger and raise a lot of money from "friends and family" who loved the story and saw another potential dot-com success story. The only thing we didn't have was a working model. It was a house of cards.

Hot Thought

> *80% of start-ups fail quickly.*

I had a very large number of shares of founder's stock which made the reverse merger very seductive. Our stock came out on the bulletin board at $0.25 in January of 2000 and climbed to

$8.25 within thirty-one days. My stock was worth nearly $5 million on paper. We thought that we were the next "dot-com darlings" and we thought our financial future was set in stone. However, our founder's stock was a Regulation D offering and therefore restricted under Rule 144. So, what does that mean? It meant at the time that we could not trade any of our shares for a twelve-month period and therefore could not take any profits. Some of our friends who bought shares on the open market were able to buy low and sell high in that thirty-one day period.

They came out smelling like a rose. Most of our friends, however, held on for the ride and the outcome wasn't as pretty. By the time the twelve-month restriction had elapsed, our dot-com had gone "dot-bomb" and the stock price was in the gutter. We never produced a working model, our story lost its appeal, and like many other investors, I had lost the money that I personally "gambled" in the wild west of dot-com mania.

My major lesson learned was that of "easy come, easy go." It's very difficult to cheat nature. It's all about energy. You don't grow an oak tree in a year and the meteoric success stories in the technology space are few and far between. As Blair Singer, Rich Dad Advisor, used to say, "Starting a business is a three- to five-year dogfight." Brad Sugars, Founder of ActionCOACH, goes one step further. He says it takes seven years to build a rock solid business. Start-ups can be very alluring and full of promise, but they are certainly not for the faint of heart!

Belief and Criticism

The most difficult part of the start-up phase, Trish McCarty says, is belief – especially if you are trying to do something that's never been done before, or could be seen as unusual. "In the beginning of trying to do something really differently everybody criticizes you. I mean, your life is really kind of miserable," Trish explains. "And in my case, and I think probably in many entrepreneurs' cases, you get to the point where you probably are completely out of money. Nobody really likes you very much. You've lost friends, relatives, and everything else." Trish says you may get to this "black moment" several times, where all the criticism starts to make you question what you are doing and your belief in yourself and your goals.

Hot Thought

> *Don't be shocked when you run out of money.*

You may ask yourself, "What have I done? Am I really doing a good job and is it ever going to pay for itself? Am I just nuts?" She says then you might start to question whether your ego is driving you, and whether or not God wants you to do this. "It's all that doubt and fear. My sweet minister friend always used to say, 'The only thing that Satan has going for him is fear.' And that's in the Bible. Satan doesn't stab you or shoot you. Satan causes fear and even if you don't agree with that analogy, it's really so ridiculous to buy into fear because you're just hoping for things to fail." Trish says by worrying and telling yourself that everything is wrong, you are causing bad stuff to happen.

Be "Done" with Fear

Trish's advice? You need to be done with fear. If you start to go into self-doubt, go for a walk, get a drink of water, or do whatever you can to keep your head from getting into a fear mindset. "It's just toxic; it doesn't do anything but make you feel terrible. It makes your brain start to react with peptides; it's a self-propelling mission." She says the more fear you have, the more fear you will have, and when fear kicks in it floods your brain with hormones that don't allow you to think straight.

The Expert Myth

"You don't have to be an expert in your area in order to generate incredible revenue," Bob Doyle says. So then what do you need to do to generate that incredible revenue? You can find the experts and consult with them. Bob says he surrounded himself with experts and immersed himself in their content. "Eventually, you will become an expert. It's about taking action and staying passionate."

Risk and Time

When you enter the start-up phase of a new venture, you're taking a risk. But what kind of risk, exactly? Brad Sugars says there are many types of risks you'll face. The first, he says is the due diligence risk. Are you buying what you think you're buying? Do you really know what you're getting into? You have to spend a great deal of time doing your due diligence, especially if you're purchasing an existing business. "Nine times out of ten, a person selling you the business has completely lied about a whole bunch of stuff," Brad warns.

The next level is industry risk. "Where is the industry going? What is the industry doing that you're buying into? Is it as I like to buy? Is it perennial? Hair dressing is a perennial; there's never going to be a day when people don't need to get their hair cut." And the third type, he says, is the risk of ability. Do you have the ability to pull it off? "That's a very big part of making sure things go right."

Most beginner entrepreneurs completely underestimate the time it takes to build a solid business. We hear the one-in-a-million, get-rich-quick success stories and are quick to view the start-up world through a pair of rose colored glasses. "It takes seven years to build a solid business. You've got to build several things. Number one is you've got to build the product and services. Second, you've got to build a team of people, and for every three employees you hire one will stay long-term and the other two will disappear if you're an average business." There's much more left to do after steps one and two are out of the way. "You've got to build retention of customers. You've got to build reputation and repeat business into the marketplace. There's a lot of things you've got to build and it takes seven years to build a good little business."

Offer What People Want

"The most difficult part of the startup phase is getting the product or service right," Brad tells me. Businesses think that they have a great product or a great service, but then no one wants to buy it. "You've got to sell what people want to buy, not what you want to sell." Brad says you have to put time and energy into getting the product or service right, priced right, and structured right before people want to buy it. "It's like, if somebody goes and buys a McDonald's franchise what are they buying? They're buying thirty to forty years of market research that tells people this is how people want to buy fries. This is how people want to buy burgers."

Hot Thought

Sell what the market *wants — not what* you *want to sell.*

Brand new businesses come in and think that their new product will sell right away, but, according to Brad, "It takes many, many moons to adjust and adapt a product or service to the point where people actually want to buy it." So ultimately, before you launch anything, do your homework. Are you going to offer something that people want? Will they start buying right away, or will there be a time investment to educate the public about your company, your brand, and your products?

Give Before You Get

You have to be prepared to put in a lot of "sweat equity" when starting up your business. "You have to give before you get," Joyce Bone says. "If you're a beginning entrepreneur, certainly use that to your favor. If you don't have money, you can bring your offer as sweat equity to the table but you better know that most people are, you know, they just don't want you to flake out on them when things don't go well or there's a bump in the road."

Sweat Equity is Good, but...

Joyce says ultimately there's more than just putting in the labor. "As I've gotten older I realize that if you're going to go with your business venture, people really need to see a financial commitment as well. You can plan on sweat equity but when you have a financial commitment to something, you stay committed." Without some form of financial commitment, anyone could just walk away. Joyce's advice? Get creative to sell sweat equity to a seasoned entrepreneur or investor. "They want to see that you've got some skin in the game."

Getting Financing

One of the most difficult parts of the start-up phase is the financing of your project. That's not a new phenomenon— Herman Cain struggled with financing in the eighties when he purchased Godfather's Pizza. "Back in 1988 when I first bought Godfather's along with my business partner, I didn't have a lot of money. We didn't have a lot of capital . . . but we were able to convince the lenders at that time – one, you didn't need but one."

Herman says they made eighteen day-long presentations to lenders before lender number nineteen said yes. "I asked the banker, 'What made you say yes?' He said, 'We were convinced that you're passionate about what it is that you're trying to do. You're passionate about what it is you're trying to do, and the other thing is you didn't have a lot of money to put down for this but as long as you lose everything before we lose a dollar we know you're going to be self motivated to succeed.' Today you can't get the bank to loan you that dollar unless you've got a dollar collateral to put up."

Cain says even if it had taken them doing one hundred presentations, they would have done every one of them.

You've Got to Convince Them

One difficulty you may face in the beginning is convincing others that your vision can be successful. Dave Liniger says his biggest difficulty in starting RE/MAX with his wife, Gail, was convincing real estate agents that their system would work. "It had never been tried in this area. When we started interviewing people in February of 1973, I ran a two-and-a-half by two-inch ad that said, 'Why split your commissions when you can keep them all to yourself? Work with us!' It was a very simple ad. I had over 1,000 phone calls and I did 204 face-to-face interviews."

Dave says they tried to recruit agents from the two major companies in town. "These two companies had an attitude that suggested it was okay for a woman to be a bookkeeper or a receptionist, but it was a man's job to sell houses. We tried to recruit those agents from those two companies, but didn't get one after five years of trying. They all said point blank, 'Well, you look awful young.' They were right, as I was twenty-seven and a lot of them were fifty and fifty-five."

The agents they interviewed were too comfortable in their current companies, and they didn't want to "rock the boat" and take a chance on this fledgling agency with its new business concept. Out of the 204 interviews they did, only four people accepted positions. "During our first five years, the majority of our agents were women. I never understood the prejudice against women. My mother was a woman, my wife was a woman, and a lot of my friends were women. I just didn't buy that philosophy."

Grow with the Job

Once you have a staff, suddenly you may have to perform a job duty you may not have done in the past. Now you're a manager in addition to being a business owner. Don't be concerned if you don't think you're a great manager at the start, but do plan to adapt to your role. It wasn't easy for Dave Liniger in the beginning. "To be quite honest with you, I was a lousy manager. I was a fairly decent leader, but I was a lousy manager. I didn't have the skill set. Fortunately, when you start a company with one agent, you don't have to have the skill set necessary to manage one hundred thousand agents forty years later. When scope of the job changes, you must grow with the job."

Do Whatever You Have to Do

Scott Goodknight also believes that getting the capital going was ones of the hardest parts of the start-up phase. Another hard part? "It's the unknown. How am I going to eat? How am I going to pay the bills?" He says one of the most humbling experiences he ever had was when at thirty-six years old, the success he had experienced with his *Biker's Atlas* went away. "I lost control of it and the industry went down and I kind of sat around for a year. I just lived off the money that I made and I was living on the high horse and I thought it was going to last forever." But the money ran out. "And when it ran out, I mean, I was at flat, I was at 'ground zero,' as they say." Scott couldn't get anything going immediately, and he didn't have any new ideas. "So I had to go take a job moving furniture.

"There's no shame in doing what you have to do. But all the time when you're doing whatever job you're doing, you need to be working on your plan and you need to—if you're working nine to five you need to be working from five to midnight on your plan." You have to take action, Scott says. You can't sit around watching TV or hanging out with your friends. "Focus all your time. Become obsessed."

Hot Thought

*There's no shame in doing what
you have to do in the beginning.*

You have to become obsessed about your idea until it becomes a brain child, Scott says. "Until it literally germinates in your mind like a seed and it sprouts, and you've got to be patient and nurture it. And you've got to keep silent about it too." Why keep silent about your idea? It's just like the story about crabs in a bucket, Scott says. If you go to any dock or sea port, look for a bucket of crabs. "They're all trying to get out of the bucket and every once in a while one will get his claw up on the edge and he'll start clawing out. What happens? The rest of them will reach up and they're trying to climb out too but what happens is they pull him back in."

It may take a few tries before you get to the point where you're ready to start your new endeavor. "I had to get knocked over the head again and again and again and just to make up my mind that I'm not going to back and work for somebody else ever."

The People Closest to You

Those crabs trying to pull you back in could be your friends or family. "In my experience, the people closest to you will try the hardest to steal your dream because they're scared for their security," Scott tells me. He says he could tell people lots of things about what they have to do and what the hardest thing is, but really, Scott says, "It's getting the belief. It's getting the faith."

If you're not worried about them trying to scare you away from your dream, you shouldn't worry about the possibility of them giving up on you because of all the long hours and stress associated with starting a new business. Because it's not going to be an issue, Scott says. "All your friends will be there and your family is going to be there. They're not going to abandon you."

Hot Seat

✓ Who do you think your biggest critics will be when you try to start up your business? Will you be able to withstand the criticism?

✓ Do you think you're an expert in the industry your new business will be in? If not, what will you to do help yourself generate maximum revenue?

✓ What risks do you see yourself facing when you start your new venture?

✓ Have you thought about how much you can invest, both in sweat equity and cash, into your new business?

✓ Are you prepared to "do whatever you have to do"? List some evidence of your determination.

STAND IN THE HEAT
Chapter Fifteen

Your BIG Venture

"Adventure without risk is Disneyland."

- Douglas Coupland
Canadian novelist

Sometimes an entrepreneur's idea can take on a life of its own and become something much bigger than originally intended. I remember George McKerrow telling me that what LongHorn Steakhouse has become is a back-handed compliment to his original vision. He envisioned having only four to five restaurants, so that he had time to play golf with his friends and drink a few beers from time to time. He surrounded himself with a great team and the rest is history.

I am a huge fan of Firehouse Subs and I love the story of how two brothers and former firefighters, Chris and Robin Sorensen, started the business. They opened their first unit in Jacksonville, Florida on a shoestring with money they borrowed from their family. They had a local artist paint a firefighter motif mural on the wall in the original shop and they served a really good product. They admit that they didn't have a grandiose business plan to conquer the world from the beginning. They didn't even have anything drawn on paper. They simply wanted to serve a better sub sandwich and be in business for themselves. Seventeen years later, they have more than four hundred fifty stores through franchising. Robin Sorensen admits on CNBC's *How I Made My Millions*, "I don't think we were smart enough to probably realize what at risk we were. The fact that we opened the first week and we had like eighty dollars left in our checking account." Not bad for a couple guys who had to work side jobs to supplement their income as full-time firefighters to make ends meet. "We never looked at it about making money for us. We just focused on how we could kick everybody's tail."

So, what will your BIG venture be? Are you adventurous and risk-tolerant enough to get started? Do you aspire to conquer the world or just be in business for yourself and call your own shots? Either desire is certainly noble. Don't be surprised, however, if your little idea someday turns into a really big venture. Your exit strategy may evolve from passing your business onto the next generation to selling to a larger entity and cashing out for the big bucks. Knowing that anything is possible in the world of business stokes the fire in my belly. With the right combination of vision, passion and sweat equity, you can start with a little idea and build your own empire. Go ahead, get started now!

Bigger Than Money

George McKerrow didn't want to start a restaurant to just make money. "My motivation was lifestyle and the freedom to be in charge of my own destiny. I wanted to own, operate, and run my own business." His original plan for LongHorn Steaks was to build a little honky-tonk restaurant. "I'd be able to have an occasional cold beer and play a little bit of golf. I could enjoy a good lifestyle and perhaps build four or five of them around town."

His other plan was to take friends he knew in the business and partner with them. "I built the first LongHorn and before the second one opened, I partnered with Bill Norman. We were going to develop Skeeter's Mesquite Grill. I partnered with an old friend in Florida and we built a restaurant down there. However, I quickly realized that this loose idea of partnerships all over the place was getting really unwieldy." So George sold out of the partnership in Florida, opened a second LongHorn and also opened Skeeter's in the same year.

Your "Success Formula"

George says they had great barbeque and a really fun concept, but they didn't really go together. "Lewis Grizzard and Hulk Hogan used to hang out there all the time. The same thing happened with Skeeter's. There was just too much diversification. I realized that once we had discovered the success formula for LongHorn, we needed to stay focused." That focus on the "success formula" led to LongHorn ultimately becoming something very different from George's original vision. "LongHorn is now everything I've said it never would be. And I don't mean that in an insulting way. What I set out to do with LongHorn was to be different. Everything it is today is exactly what I said it never would be." But, George says, that's not why he is not there today. And, "That's also why it's a highly successful, publicly traded company, owned by the largest restaurant company in the world."

Hot Thought

> *When you find something that works, stick with it!*

Humility

Great entrepreneurs are famous for starting things, but not necessarily finishing. I believe it takes a different skill set to start a venture as opposed to guiding it through the operational stage. George agrees with that. "I'll tell you that one of the biggest compliments I ever got from the business community, Wall Street, and the bankers, was that I knew when to get out of the way." In 2000 George retired from the company he built, RARE Hospitality International, which owned LongHorn and The Capital Grille. He then went on to partner with Ted Turner to open Ted's Montana Grill in 2002. The company now has over forty locations in more than sixteen states. He remains humble about the massive success he has had in his career.

Early Challenges

Brad Sugars's big venture was started by accident, he says. Brad had been speaking at seminars by request, and started getting asked to do consulting and coaching. Brad may have sort of fallen into his new role, but it wasn't without challenges. "Let's be realistic. There's no such thing as a business that gets off the ground without challenges. I was not out inventing a business. I was inventing an industry." Brad says that when he told people that he was a business coach, they said, "What the heck's a business coach?"

"The hardest business in the world is one where you have to educate the marketplace as to what your entire product or service is. The easiest business in the world is shoes. Everyone buys them. Everyone wears them. You just got to come up with a better way of selling them." Brad says Zappos.com's founders, Tony Hsieh and Nick Swinmurn, did just that. They created a billion dollar business in ten years. "They did a lot of hard work and did a lot of things right in the middle but, you know, to me that's a very important aspect of business success."

New Ideas Breed Controversy

Dave Liniger was motivated to build RE/MAX to enable real estate agents to take home better commissions. At the time, Dave says ordinary real estate companies were splitting their commissions with their agents on a 50/50 basis. The agents were getting 50 percent, but had to pay transportation, travel, and realtor fees, so they were netting less. "Ultimately, 80 percent of the people who got a real estate license would quit in less than a year. It was a very tough business with no salaries or draws." It would take an agent months to learn the business, and doing that with no salary was difficult. Agents would try to work for the biggest company in town, but then would end up starting their own real estate office.

"The attitude was, 'I could make a much bigger portion of the commission by not giving up 50 percent if I went into business for myself.' This trend ended the spinning wheel of agents coming in and dropping out of the business and new agents moving up to the biggest company and then leaving to start their own companies." Dave says in the Denver market in 1973, there were about ten large players that had 50 percent of the market share, and one thousand small, "mom and pop" shops owned the balance of the market. He decided to set up a company that would work on the basis of a co-op. Doctors, dentists, lawyers, and architects were already doing it – sharing the same facilities, secretaries, and assistants. They would pay a share of the expenses and keep all of their commissions.

Dave would be going against the grain of how things were done in the real estate industry at the time. While most real estate companies were focusing on the real estate customer, he was focusing on the agent. "We were interested in attracting the experienced agent who could have been in business for themselves anyway." Dave says the approach was very controversial at the time.

Once they opened, Dave says the industry absolutely hated them. "The powerful companies could see that if we succeeded and paid our people, they would lose a lot of their agents to us. So, the powerful companies did everything they could. They tried to have us thrown out of the Board of Realtors and off the Multiple Listing Services."

Hot Thought

> *Know your ultimate customer.*

The First Three to Five Years

Starting RE/MAX certainly came with a number of challenges in the first few years. "We made several major mistakes in the beginning. The first mistake was starting the company in a recession." In addition to competing with powerful companies, the company was starting in rough financial times. Dave says he didn't fully understand what a recession was. "I just knew that people wanted to buy houses and people wanted to sell houses. So, we just started." Another major setback was that the investor group backing them pulled out just three weeks after they opened the offices.

"We began in a tremendous financial crunch. Then we had the oil embargo and the oil crisis. People were waiting in lines at filling stations for a half an hour to get five gallons of gas. Talk about trial by fire!" Dave says the first two to three years were unbelievably challenging. "It took five years before we really turned around and became profitable where we could pay off our debt." But the company went from that one office in Denver to a now having offices around the globe.

Hot Thought

> *"Starting a new business is a three to five year dog fight!"* —
> *Blair Singer, Rich Dad Advisor to Robert Kiyosaki*

Kids and Entrepreneurship

Trish McCarty, who founded StarShine Academy, a K-12 school for high-risk, inner-city children in Phoenix, says that starting a school was originally not on her radar. Trish had worked for AT&T, Mellon Bank, and Norwest. "I made really good money and I got to stay in the nicest places and go to the nicest resorts. I really had a nice life and I really thought I was doing good work. I was helping a lot of people with their banking."

Starting the Academy, she says, was a progression of many things. Trish's father, who was in the Air Force, raised her family outside of the United States. He felt that if his children were raised outside of the country then they would love it as much as he did. Her father was always worried about the education system in this country. "He said that we are not learning at the speed of other countries and we're not gonna stay up on our edge of being the greatest country if we didn't get our education fixed." Trish says that as time went on she got more and more worried about our children not learning what they needed to be good human beings. "The more I saw kids just being total brats in the grocery store and parents that didn't have a clue as to how to be a good parent—doing the best they could, struggling but completely ineffective—I knew it all had to do with what you know." Parents were doing the best they could with the knowledge they have. Trish says she kept seeing this issue over and over, and began to think that the country was probably into three generations of bad parenting.

Hot Thought

> *Instill in your children the spirit of our Founding Fathers.*

Then tragedy struck the nation on September 11, 2011. "It just devastated me. I mean, I know a lot of people feel the same way I did. It was pretty devastating to the whole country, but I felt as sorry for the people flying into those towers as I did the people in the towers because I thought nobody in their right mind would want to kill that many people and kill themselves and smash into a side of a building if they'd been raised right or taught right." Trish believes the terrorists were taught with fear, dread, anger, and all the things that pre-program a person's brain to carry out that type of behavior. "I knew that could be unlearned. I knew it." So she started talking about it. "We have a crisis in America. The economy is going to remain in a state of decline if we don't start teaching our kids to be good entrepreneurs and respect the tenets of our Founding Fathers."

The more Trish started speaking to groups about the original ideas in the Declaration of Independence and the Bill of Rights being lost, the more people started saying that something needed to be done about it. Then she got her chance. "An Episcopal priest who had been a long-term friend of mine called me and she said, 'I'm going to make your dreams come true. We've got a building that's owned by the Diocese that is on the worst drive-by shooting street in Phoenix and you can prove your point and open a school.' I just about fell over." And after a series of roadblocks, Trish opened up the StarShine Academy.

She says in StarShine, they have proven that the most important thing for success is self-discipline and getting along with others. "If you don't have those two things you will not be a success. If you do have those two things you will find your way to some level of success." She also believes in the three things she says filter all human judgment and eventually filter what happens to you: "Am I lovable? Am I relevant? Am I significant?"

"I'm not doing StarShine just to be a nice person. I'm doing StarShine because I am worried about our children. I'm worried about the United States. When 9/11 happened I thought we were gonna lose our country because I figured as long as there's one mean person out there they're gonna make all of our lives miserable." Trish says she's trying to create a system that will pay for itself and produce money to open more schools, so that education is not dependent on dollars. "We should be able to figure this out, because every single child on the planet needs the very best education we can find. I'm doing this as an entrepreneurial thing. I keep saying I want to be the first billionaire out of education. There's never been a woman billionaire in this field."

Hot Seat

✓ Are you hoping to start a business because of the lure of money? Or for other reasons? It's okay to be honest with yourself!

✓ What led you to your "big idea"? Was it from a personal need? Something you think society needs?

✓ What do you think your early challenges will be when you start your business?

✓ Is your idea something that will be controversial in its industry? Will you face criticism or tough competition from others in the industry?

STAND IN THE HEAT
Chapter Sixteen

Listen to Your Customers

"If you work just for money, you'll never make it, but if you love what you're doing and you always put the customer first, success will be yours."

- Ray Kroc
McDonald's

I believe one of the most underutilized skills in human endeavor is the willingness and ability to effectively listen. As a matter of fact, my two largest pet peeves in life are people who interrupt and people who litter. If you want to instantly kill bonding and rapport with another person, continuously interrupt their communication.

My favorite new comedian is Brian Regan and he brilliantly labels offensive interrupters as "Me Monsters." If you want to enjoy some great comic spin on the subject, go to YouTube and do a search for "Brian Regan dinner party." I guarantee you will get a chuckle from his delivery and immediately think of someone close to you who is guilty of being a "Me Monster."

In the mid 1990s I worked for a company in Atlanta that sold customer service and customer retention programs to the retail industry. I was amazed to learn that it typically costs five to six times more money to keep an existing customer than it does to acquire a new customer. I also had a paradigm shift about complaints. Most people will tell eight to ten people about a bad experience, but they will tell far fewer people about a good experience. What does that say about our society? People love dirty laundry!

If handled correctly, a complaint is a golden opportunity to turn a dissatisfied customer into a loyal, lifetime customer. Most people simply want to be heard and understood. Most people don't complain because they don't like confrontation. Therefore, they simply go away.

I believe we should listen to our customers and our potential customers—our prospects in the marketplace. Often entrepreneurs will put extensive time and energy into creating products and services that they are passionate about without accurately determining what the market really wants. Who is your target market? What do your customers want in your products and services?

Great Service

Many of you probably babysat a neighbor or relative's kids to make some cash as a teen. And depending on the kids you were watching, it may have been easy money. Lisa Levison babysat too, but she decided to take it to another level. "I went out and really promoted myself as a babysitter at a time when people were just paying by the hour," she says. "I was one of the first people in the neighborhood to start scheduling and also charging for every head. If I brought food then that would be another service that I was bringing in. I would always bring little care packages, that sort of thing." Lisa made sure to try to land some good babysitting gigs. "I always pushed for those beach trips where I could go and take care of the children while they were at the beach, and even help them with getting box lunches ready for the beach as well." Lisa says that from the beginning, she understood the importance of service. "People will always pay for good service, especially when they know things are going to be done right." She says the drive to be an entrepreneur came more from instinct than from observing others. "I come from a family of engineers, so I didn't get it from them."

Customer Expectations

How important is customer service today? "Critical, critical, critical!" says Herman Cain. "Because the competition is tougher, the environment is tougher, the economy is tougher, and the only thing that you have that you can distinguish your product or service from anybody else is that level of service." Herman says anyone can replicate the quality of a product, but it's more difficult for them to replicate your service culture. "In every business that I was involved in, every business that I took over to turn around, I had a very simple service philosophy: exceed customer's expectations. Not meet but exceed." Fifty years ago, he says, all you needed to do was the meet the customer's expectations. But today, "To be successful in business as an entrepreneur you've got to have a philosophy and a culture within your company of exceeding customer's expectations."

Hot Thought

At all times exceed your customers' expectations.

Embrace Their Ideas

Your customers can give you some great ideas, if you're listening and you're receptive. When you hear RE/MAX, what do you picture? That red and blue hot air balloon, right? Well the company's logo wasn't the idea of co-founder Dave Liniger or his wife, Gail. The idea came from some of their Albuquerque franchisees who thought it would be a great gimmick for charity walk-a-thons and RE/MAX office grand openings. "We eventually embraced the idea," Dave says. "The logo became so successful that we added it to our signs and business cards. It has become the most recognizable real estate logo in the world."

Earn the Right Everyday

RE/MAX's customers are their agents, more so than the homebuyers or homeowners looking to sell. "Most real estate companies focus on the real estate customer. We were interested in attracting the experienced agent who could have been in business for themselves anyway. We provide the training, motivation, planning, and goal-setting. The average agent in RE/MAX has been in the business thirteen years, so we don't have the big mill of part-timers and beginners."

RE/MAX's approach was very controversial at the time. While today most people will say that the philosophy is great, Dave tells me there weren't many positive comments at the start. "The people at the major competitors badmouthed me and called me a 'piranha.' I was a 'thief stealing everybody's agents.' That was their attitude. Well, slavery's been gone for a long time.

"Companies don't own their agents, they employ their agents. At a real estate company, your only asset is your people. It's not like a grocery store or a sporting goods store where you have inventory. You have people. Your asset walks out the door every night at five-thirty or six o'clock. Whether they walk back in the next day is up to you. As a manager you provide for them an environment where they want to return."

What are you going to do to keep your customers coming back to you? Find ways to bring them back to your business, instead of letting them head for your competition.

Hot Thought

> *Be open minded to*
> *constructive criticism.*

"Your Baby is Ugly"

While getting advice from other entrepreneurs is going to be helpful, what you really need to do, Wendy Reed believes, is to listen to your customers more. "If you're struggling, it probably has to do with your product. If you're not bringing in enough money there's probably something 'off' on your offering, so go to the customers. Be open-minded enough to let the market call your baby ugly."

HEAT Moment

> *Wendy Reed showed*
> *Tenacity when she listened to*
> *her customers, made*
> *adjustments, and persevered*
> *to build a great company.*

You have to use your customers as your advisory board, Wendy says. "People ask for advice and then they spend all their time defending what they did. Okay, well who cares what you did. It doesn't matter what happened before. It's irrelevant; it's unproductive. Let's talk about how you are going to get to the next place." She says if you're struggling as an entrepreneur, you have to define where you are. Talk to people and see what they'd like you to do. If they tell you things you don't want to hear, if they "call your baby ugly" then, "you have to just suck it down and listen to what they're saying because they're trying to help you." Get their input, and then figure out what do to about it. This means that you are going to have to put your ego aside, an ability every entrepreneur should have. "It's not about you. It's about how you move forward and you can't do that if you can't get past your ego."

Hot Seat

✓ Think of past instances where you have provided great service. What did you do, and what made it great?

✓ Picture your future self running your new business. Can you see yourself meeting customer expectations? Can you see yourself exceeding them?

✓ Will you be receptive to ideas from customers? Can you think of a time where someone gave you a new idea and you implemented it? It doesn't have to be work-related, it could be in your personal life.

✓ Have you ever had someone "call your baby ugly"? How did it make you feel? Did you let it get to you, or did you take action to make things better?

STAND IN THE HEAT
Chapter Seventeen

Biggest Lesson Learned

"Experience is a hard teacher because she gives the test first, the lesson afterward."

- Vernon Law
Major League Baseball pitcher

My late uncle Jim Harrell used to say, "When you stall, you lose." Most of us have had several good ideas in our lifetime that were worthy of going to market, but we stalled and didn't take action due to some level of fear. Worse yet, many of us have seen somebody else go to market with the same idea and capitalize! My biggest lesson learned in business is that the best idea in the world is useless if you don't take immediate action in the moment of truth. Moments of inspiration can be fleeting, so we have to do something in those moments to start the process of momentum.

A few years ago I was studying internet marketing strategies from one of the "gurus" in the industry, Matt Bacak. I was attending one of his events in Atlanta and he said something that really hit me between the eyes. He said that when he and his colleagues are about to launch a new product online, they never wait until they feel the product is perfect. They launch the product when they feel it is 70 percent perfect and let the marketplace tell them what needs to be fixed or improved. Matt and his colleagues don't suffer "paralysis of analysis" as they understand that an imperfect plan massively implemented is better than a perfect plan that sits on the shelf.

Hot Thought

When you stall you lose!

I have seen several ideas I had over the past twenty years be brought to market by someone else who had the guts, capital, and perspiration to turn an idea into reality. How many times have you said to yourself, "What if?" What if I had listened to my instinct and taken action on that idea? Where would I be now? Well, the good news is that it's never too late. Paul Zane Pilzer wrote a great book entitled, *Unlimited Wealth*. In his book he suggests that there is unlimited wealth in the world because there are unlimited ideas. The only limit to what we can create is our own imagination. Albert Einstein said, "Logic will get you from A to B. Imagination will take you everywhere."

What lessons have you learned in your business life? Have those lessons chained you to the ground in fear or have they motivated you to take massive action? Will you lie on your deathbed with regret asking yourself that painful question, "What if?" or will you act in those fleeting moments of inspiration? Remember, when you stall you lose!

Your Team Will Build Your Business

Brad Sugars has learned more about himself along his path from a twenty-year-old in business to managing a global empire. "Your ability to manage grows with time as long as you keep taking on new knowledge," he says. He also says he couldn't have gotten where he is now without some help along the way. Brad made sure that he always had great people on his team. "You'll never build a great business without great people because they actually build the business."

The Fight

Joyce Bone had to work on her skills in dealing with bullies, whether on the playground or in the boardroom. "If someone is trying to take advantage of me or push me around, I get nose to nose and I give it right back to them. I never have tolerated bullies in my life."

When Joyce was a child, she had to stand up for her siblings, against kids who were teasing them. Her favorite story involves her Raggedy Ann lunchbox. She and her sister were walking home with a third grade classmate of her sister. The third grader started hitting Joyce's sister in the face, and Joyce says she warned the girl to stop or Joyce would make her stop. "And, of course, I'm in kindergarten so she wasn't very intimidated, so she just kept wailing on my sister so I took my lunch box—which back in those days were made out of metal—and I took it and I just clocked her upside the head as hard as I could and I sent her just sprawling across the ground." The girl took off and ran home. The next day, Joyce got called to the principal's office with her sister and the bully. "The principal, he just kind of winked at me and he just said, 'Joyce, you cannot beat people up with your lunch box, are we clear?' And I'm like, 'Okay.' He's like, 'Okay, go back to class.'"

HEAT Moment

> *Joyce Bone exercised bold Enthusiasm when she clocked her sister's attacker upside the head with a heavy, metal Raggedy Ann lunchbox.*

Joyce says as a child that she had to defend herself, or her siblings, in that way. Once she got into the corporate environment, Joyce says, while working in male-dominated industries, she was sometimes bullied by men. "A couple of times I was bullied by men and I just stuck it to them, and got in their face. I outwitted them. I've have always been a fighter out of necessity more than anything else. I'm a pretty tough cookie now."

Bullying in the workplace can come in all forms. "It might not be as overt as some of the situations I've found myself in but there are people who will continually ask, ask, ask and just be a time-sucker in your life. They may not be a bully per se but they're taking advantage of you. You have to learn how to protect yourself and the important people around you."

Momentum

Kathleen Hall has learned you can believe in fate and luck, but you can't just sit back when good things start to happen, you have to work even harder. "What I see with a lot of entrepreneurs is when that 'moment' happens, they'll rest on their laurels or kind of stall and go, 'Wow, this is really great; I'm just going to enjoy this.' No, that's the time you work the hardest."

Dr. Hall says after she wrote her first book, the next thing she knew she was on the *Today Show*. She got a call, they flew her to New York and put her in a beautiful hotel, and there she was on the show and meeting people. But she didn't relax after that first big interview. "On the plane on the way back I did a whole PR schedule and a whole media thing of where I was going to go next. What the press release was going to be. What the pitch was going to be." Then she was on Martha Stewart's show. "And when I was there I talked to the producers. I became friends with the producers and I would ask them questions. People that were in the green room with me – I was just a sponge. And that's the way to do it."

She says instead of thinking that things will happen in the way that dominoes fall—where one thing takes care of the next thing, making everything move by itself—she made things happen. "I took every single domino and planned the next move. Once that opportunity opens or luck or fate or whatever happens that's when you work."

Hot Thought

When you see an opportunity, take immediate action.

Reaching for the Sky

A couple of years after RE/MAX started using a hot air balloon for a logo, Dave Liniger's friend came to him with a big idea. Chauncey Dunne suggested they use a giant helium balloon that goes up thousands of feet and hang a gondola from it. Dave says Chauncey told him, "'If you could launch it successfully and get up to 120,000 feet, you'd be way over the weather. You'd never have thunderstorms and it would just be surviving for a three week time period.'" Chauncey asked Dave if he'd be interested in sponsoring something like that. Eventually Dave said "Yes," if he could be one of the pilots.

But, sadly, Chauncey's wife was diagnosed with breast cancer and passed away six years later, so they never worked on the idea. Then in 1997, Dave says there were lots of unsuccessful attempts by people to fly around the world in a balloon. "I kept thinking, 'You know, Chauncey's idea would work.' So, we started getting involved and ended up with 1,600 scientists as volunteers. We went from Johnson Space Center, to jet propulsion laboratories, to NASA, and we researched weather balloons. We got together and decided, 'Yeah, let's build a space capsule!'" Their project would be the first privately built space capsule in the world.

Dave says what started out as a very simple plan became very complex. He couldn't buy a space suit in the United States, so he went to Moscow and trained with cosmonauts. "We had custom space suits made for the three of us that were going to make the attempt."

During Christmas of 1998, they went to Alice Springs in Australia. They had a four week launch window. During that window, Alice Springs had the highest winds and the most rain in the desert that they had in history. They were finally able to try for a launch one day when the sky seemed clearer, Dave says. "The scientists wheeled us out onto the runway and got the balloon ready to inflate. We were standing by and had a launch window, and the scientists were counting us down. They said, 'All right. We need five more minutes.'" But they never launched. They would have sailed right into a thunderstorm that had moved into the area.

"It was daybreak as they started wheeling us back in. We got unbuckled and looked out our tiny little porthole. Twenty thousand people had come from hundreds of miles, pitched tents and camped out that night when they had heard that we were going launch. They had huge signs up posted on the fences around the airport in support of our adventure."

And before they knew it, the launch window of time was over. "Nobody saw me cry, but I did cry," Dave says. The company took a vote with officers and regional owners, and voted to try it again, but six months later re-voted and the idea was scrapped. "It was a fabulous, once in a lifetime adventure for me. Unfortunately, you don't succeed at everything you try. But as everybody says, I'm still alive."

HEAT Moment

Dave Liniger displayed passionate Enthusiasm when he attempted to fly around the planet in a hot air balloon.

Providing for Others

Lisa Levison says when she first started becoming successful, it was sort of a "me, me, me" feeling for her. But today, she says, it's "we, we, we." She says when you first start getting the money that comes with success you start thinking about what you need and think that if you can have certain things then you'll be a better person. But that's not reality for her today. "We need to all really take care of ourselves and each other. There's so much more than the 'me' and just the inner soul." Lisa says when you're giving to others, it's going to come back to you twofold. "I realized that I felt better about doing things not just for me but doing things to improve others' lives, and by giving and sharing and opening my eyes up to what was out there and what I could do and how I could benefit I actually found more fulfillment than I ever got with the 'me, me, me.'" She says now, she doesn't ever want to go back to that "me, me, me" of only looking out for herself.

HEAT Moment

Lisa Levison showed great Honor for her team when she shifted her mindset from "Me" to "We."

Hot Seat

✓ Are you reasons for wanting to go into business for yourself based on "me, me, me" or "we, we, we"? Why?

✓ Do you think that you can be successful on your own, without having a "team" around you to help you?

✓ What is a skill you had as a child that can carry over from the playground to the board room?

✓ What's your plan for making the dominoes move? Are you hoping to sit back and let them fall after the first one is tipped over?

STAND IN THE HEAT
Chapter Eighteen

What's Next?

"Vision is the art of seeing the invisible."

- Jonathon Swift, Author
Gulliver's Travels

Near the end of the interview, I asked all of these incredible entrepreneurs a powerful, two-part question: "Have you fulfilled your vision for yourself?" and "What's next?" It came as no surprise that none of these individuals had fulfilled their ultimate vision of themselves; they feel there is plenty more to accomplish in their lifetime. Nobody was satisfied and resting on their laurels and prior achievements. Everyone had an even greater vision for the future and they were focused on, and committed to making that vision a reality.

The human being is a goal-oriented mechanism. Rarely do we seem to be satisfied with our station in life no matter how much we have achieved, especially when it comes to material possessions. Most of the entrepreneurs in this book who have achieved a large degree of financial success seemed to be looking for the next level. I will call that next level "significance."

There is a major difference between success and significance. Success is primarily selfish and defined by material possessions, personal achievements, and financial statements. Significance on the other hand is selfless. Significance is when we are focused outside of ourselves and our energies are directed toward the improvement of mankind. I would imagine that anyone who is reading this book is interested in experiencing a higher level of success in their life and in the lives of their families. I also believe that many people with the entrepreneurial spirit are greatly interested in transcending success and moving into significance.

It is said that success typically precedes significance. You can have success without significance, but you cannot have significance without success. I would agree. If we look at psychologist Abraham Maslow's hierarchy of needs, security and belonging are certainly on lower levels than self-actualization. Most of us will probably never realize self-actualization or significance until we have climbed beyond security and success on the ladder of life.

As for myself, my dream is to realize success and significance simultaneously. All I want to do is help millions of people worldwide realize their greatest potential through my speaking, writing, and live events. As a result, I want to experience financial independence for my family. Hey, is that too much to ask?

Have a Bigger Vision than Yourself

Herman Cain plans to make a difference. "Today I'm all about helping other people fulfill their vision," he says. Herman says he has exceeded his vision for himself, and he is now working on his vision for others. "To make a big difference in their lives on as many people as I can in the area of where I can bring the most to the party. Today, that's being on the radio and helping people learn and become aware of the facts so they can make more intelligent, better-informed decisions." Herman, who for a time in 2011 was the GOP's frontrunner for the presidential nomination, is on News-Talk WSB Radio in Atlanta on a daily basis. He had taken a break from radio after being a nighttime host on WSB Radio in Atlanta for about three years.

Lisa Levison's vision hasn't fulfilled her vision for herself yet, because that vision extends beyond just her abilities. "When I'm close is the day that I walk in and see my son running one of my companies and doing a better job than I did."

Think Globally, Act Locally

Trish McCarty says she won't have fulfillment until "Every single kid on the planet has the very best tools and education at their fingertips at all times." Trish's StarShine Academy started in Phoenix, but is going global. Trish says they did training for teachers in Africa that was the largest teacher training that had ever been done in the country before. "We had eight hundred teachers for three days in Liberia. Nothing like that had ever been done. I literally, in that three days, I watched the country completely change, because they were given empowerment ideas and tools." She says the teachers were taught how to get along with each other, how to pick up trash. "They just didn't know what they didn't know."

Trish says her company is rolling out a franchise system that will allow people to have a StarShine "school in a box." "We've got private schools that are going to convert to StarShine because they need to leverage what they have. They need to be able to buy equipment at a better price. They need to be able to have a research team constantly researching the latest, greatest 'brain stuff' so there are people that are wanting to convert just so they can be a part of a team."

There are schools that StarShine is supporting in Sudan, Liberia, and Kenya that don't have any money. Trish says they need to figure out other ways to bring supplies to those schools so that the kids there can have the same level of training that children in the United States will get. "Then we are hoping to be in all fifty states, the UK, Canada, Australia, and India all on the same day. We literally will open up those franchises overnight so there's a lot of preparation going on right now to make sure that we've got the grid system set up." They even want mothers who are homeschooling to be able to access the same tools the schools will be using. "Providing StarShine school in a box will give them a way to train their kids the way they want to with high accreditation. We have international and national accreditation, so once you plug into StarShine you have an accredited system so the kids can have an accredited certificate when they get through." They have a lot of planning and work ahead of them, but Trish is excited about all the partnerships happening globally.

Give More than You Take

George McKerrow was extremely successful with LongHorn Steaks, and today, he says, he is fulfilled in his life. "I think that I've given back more than I've taken out. I've helped more people than I've taken from. I've helped a lot of people become successful and I'm really proud of that." He says he's also given back to the world in many ways and continues to do that. But, he says "I'm not finished yet."

Hot Thought

Leave the world a better place than you found it.

He and partner Ted Turner both want to grow Ted's Montana Grill more. "We've created a brand that we're proud of," George says. "However, Ted's Montana Grill hasn't been as successful as it can be. That's still my mission." He says he'd like to see the restaurant chain become a highly respected and successful brand, and then hand it off to someone in the next five to ten years who can take it to the same level as LongHorn.

Entrepreneurs Rarely "Retire"

Like many successful entrepreneurs who no longer need to work to earn a paycheck to survive, George says he's too young to retire. "I tried that once," he says. "I retired and sailed and hunted and skied and fished, and I had a great time, but I was bored." George says he gets to do those things anyway. What he really wants these days is to continue to have a voice. He is working to make sure that no children go to school hungry. "We need our governors and our states to get more active than they are because seventy percent of kids who go to school in Georgia have their first meal at ten a.m. We can do better than that."

He wants to continue that effort, and to continue to have fun. "I think business is fun and I enjoy traveling the world and starting new ideas." George says he even invented a chicken cooker with a friend of his, and they're selling them worldwide. "It's a small company, but it's cool to have a patent and a product that you have invented." Launching new ideas never gets old to an entrepreneur.

Stay Fresh Through Adventure

Dave Liniger says he has definitely not fulfilled his vision for himself. Dave quotes from a Zig Zigler motivational speech, "'When you're green, you're growing, and when you're ripe, you rot.'" Dave says that since starting RE/MAX, he has evolved as a businessman and a human being. "People change and they change constantly."

Dave says a person's evolutionary process changes as they grow. "My personal accomplishments are not nearly as important to me anymore as passing on a wealth of experience to the next generation. I have always taken a great deal of pleasure in being an adventurer, and my dreams, desires, and adventures started as a child." Dave had many dreams. He wanted to be in the military, he wanted to be a cop, a pilot, a big game hunter; to fly airplanes, skydive, and scuba dive. "That's what I've done with my entire life. Everybody pegs me with founding RE/MAX. To keep from burning out, I've kept myself fresh with hundreds of adventures all over the world. My thing has always been turning people on to things that they have never done before."

He has probably certified over fifty of his friends at RE/MAX as scuba divers, and then taken them on diving adventures around the world. "I woke them up to new things. When I drove NASCAR for ten years, I took twenty of my officers to various driving schools. I got them behind the wheel for three and four days at speeds up to one hundred and sixty miles an hour. I challenged them!" Dave says sharing the things he was passionate about with others on these adventures revitalized him. "As I continue to mature, it becomes more important to me to pass on the wisdom that I have gathered from my mentors. I want to help people have a different perspective of the world than they had before they met me."

Vision Boards

Sometimes, not everything will work out as planned, even if it seems you are on a sure path. Joyce Bone says that she didn't fulfill her vision completely, but she fulfilled the parts that she could control.

She is always creating new visions to work towards. "Every year I put up a new vision board and I put pictures and I write goals for myself every year. I re-write goals all year long and I'm always tweaking my focus." It's hard for Joyce to completely relax, especially as the mother of three children. "You're always busy so it's hard to kind of get that space for yourself. So my latest vision is to create space for myself where I have time where I'm not interrupted and I can think; so more getaways are my vision."

From a business standpoint, Joyce says she would like for Millionaire Moms to provide more information that is "from the streets"—from people that have actually been there and have been successful at it. "My goal is to just kind of streamline what I've been doing and only do the things that people really resonate with and that I enjoy doing."

HEAT Moment

Dave Liniger expands the lives of others by introducing them to adventurous Action.

Be Comfortable With the Unknown

Scott Goodknight hopes to grow his Mental M.A.P.S. community to a community of millions of people all over the world that are supporting each other in achieving their outcomes. But other than that hope, Scott says he doesn't know what's next. "And that kind of contradicts what I say about knowing your outcomes all the time. I don't know what's going to happen in this world. And I don't know what's going to happen with the people around me. And I don't know what's going to happen with me. And I think that that's okay."

Hot Thought

> *Become comfortable being uncomfortable.*

Scott says as an entrepreneur you've got to be okay with the unknown. He compares it to the journey of Christopher Columbus. "They didn't know if they were going to sail off the edge of the earth. They had a plan and they started sailing west. They sailed into the unknown, and so your life is going to stay the same if all you do is stay in the know." You've got to get into the unknown, spend some time in there, and get comfortable with it.

Growing or Dying

Bob Doyle says his vision for himself is always in progress. "As soon as I develop one vision, like 'Let's start a business, let's make it successful,' great. 'Now what?' I've got this money thing figured out; I've got a business going. I want to put myself out in the world a little bit bigger so I took that on." Now, Bob says his passion is getting people out of their heads creatively. "Showing them the benefits of doing something equivalent to picking up a ukulele and getting over yourself, and how powerful the experience of life can be." Bob is cultivating the idea for workshops.

"If you're not constantly growing and creating new ideas and visions for yourself, then sooner or later you will plateau and have that death feeling. You don't want to go, 'Is this all there is?' No it's, 'Yeah! We did this and now what's next for me?'" It's a feeling you might get in a job that you've been in for too long.

Bob wants to find new ways to have the same kind of impact, helping people to live their lives powerfully and abundantly. It's the same end result he has always wanted for people, but, "Now it's just I'm going to be doing it in a different way that's more fun for me, that causes me to step outside my comfort zone more and expand and share my own creativity and see where that leads me down that road too."

Hot Seat

✓ Have you extended your vision beyond yourself yet? What happens after you "get there" and have met your goals? What will be next?

✓ How can your company or venture extend beyond the United States? Do you see it "going global"?

✓ Do you think you will ever "retire"? Are you the type who will always want to have something new to do?

✓ Will you embrace the unknown after you launch your new venture, or are you the type of person who has to have the next step planned out ahead of time?

STAND IN THE HEAT
Chapter Nineteen

Giving Back

"Remember that the happiest people are not those getting more, but those giving more."

**- H. Jackson Brown, Jr.
Author, *Life's Little Instruction Book***

Martin Luther King said, "Everybody can be great...because anybody can serve. You don't have to have a college degree to serve. You don't have to make your subject and verb agree to serve. You only need a heart full of grace. A soul generated by love." I will be the first person to admit that I have room for growth when it comes to service and giving back. Although I'm willing give a dollar here or a dollar there to the Shriners Hospital for Children, the Girl Scouts in front of the grocery store, or the occasional beggar, I don't give back nearly enough. Consequently, I am greatly inspired by the level of giving by some of the entrepreneurs in this book.

I believe the reason that most of us don't give back more in the form of time or money is fear. We tend to get stuck in a scarcity mindset. "How can I give money when I'm barely paying my bills?" How can I serve my community when there aren't enough hours in the day to balance my family and work life as it is?" Ironically, if we served and gave back more on a consistent basis; we would probably experience a compound effect in our financial lives that would free up more of our time. I say probably because I know that I need to serve and give back more myself. As the saying goes, "If you want to learn something, teach a class on it."

My chosen form of giving back is in the form of passing on the wisdom, philosophy, and strategies of those who have gone before me and succeeded. Thus, you are reading this book. I find that I am the happiest and most fulfilled in my core when I communicate and contribute to the lives of others. I have learned so much from the mentors I have studied, that I want to spend the rest of my life paying it forward and giving back.

I am clear that we don't have to give back an inordinate amount of time or money in order to have an impact on someone else's life. I am also clear that time is more important than money as time is the only resource that we cannot recover. Money is literally everywhere, but there are only so many hours in a day. I remember hearing the story of Elton John's mother wanting to spend more time with him. Although he has millions upon millions of dollars, she wasn't interested in his money. She was interested in sharing his ultimate resource: his time.

My son was born on November 21, 2009. At the time I was between income streams and my bank account was on vapors. Financially, I was stressed and worried. On the flip side of the coin, I was able to spend every moment of the holidays with my wife and newborn son. It was one of the greatest times of my life!

Speaking of money being everywhere, I have developed what I believe to be a wonderful habit over the past year. Whenever I see a penny on the ground, I pick it up and express sincere gratitude for it showing up in my life. The fact that it is merely a penny does not matter. It's the gratitude that matters. The gratitude creates the space for more money to flow into our lives and the more money that flows into our lives the more money we can give back!

Driven to Make a Difference

A few years ago, Dave Liniger did something really cool as a way to give back. He purchased a very special Hummer; the proceeds from that purchase went to charity. The Hummer had been used by CNN film crews; it was the first civilian Hummer to go into Baghdad. It had been shot to pieces and blown up, and then shipped back to the United States. Dave says one of those TV shows where the remake cars rebuilt the Hummer, adding things like a huge flat screen TV and boom boxes. But the most interesting thing about it was the paint job. "It looks like camouflage until you get up next to it. When you get next to it, however, it is a collection of portraits. The portraits were the memories of those four reporters and film crew had of their Iraqi invasion experience."

Dave talked to the reporters to get each of the stories of the portraits. One is of two bald marines holding each other and

219

crying. That was from an incident where a suicide bomber had killed eight marines in a mess tent. He says he will vividly remember this story all his life. A sleeping bag was painted on the hood. The reporters said their camera man had gotten stung by scorpions during the trip, and refused to ever sleep on the ground again, so he slept on the hood of the truck every night. "You don't understand all the portraits until you start looking at them and hear the stories of the campaign this Hummer had been through."

The auction house was hoping to get a quarter of a million dollars for the Hummer. One hundred percent of the proceeds, including the auctioneer's fees, would go to the Fisher House. The Fisher House builds housing for military families at military hospitals so they can live in a house next to the military hospital while their loved one is healing. Dave says he got into a bidding war, and told his auctioneer, Amy, that he was going to get the Hummer for sure. And, "She started crying. I asked her why she was crying and she said her brother was in Iraq at that time. The bidding war got up to about $800,000 and she whispered in my ear 'Why don't you jump to a million and see if we can shove this guy out of the bid?'"

So Dave raised his bid to a million dollars. The guy he was bidding against looked up at the other auctioneers and asked to stop the bidding. Then, Dave says, "He walked up on the stage where I was and said, 'Who the hell are you and what are you going to do with this Hummer?'" Dave told the man who he was, and his plan to put the Hummer on tour through the United States to raise awareness about what is happening to wounded soldiers, and to try to raise money for the Walter Reed Army Medical Center and the Fisher Foundation. And what happened next? "He looked at the auctioneer and he said, 'I tell you what. Let Mr. Liniger have the car. I'll write the first $250,000 donation to the Fisher Foundation.'"

Dave got the Hummer, and put the car on tour for three years. It was a hit everywhere it traveled.

HEAT Moment

> *Dave Liniger displayed selfless Honor when he uniquely raised money for the Walter Reed Army Medical Center and the Fisher Foundation.*

Giving Back: A Company-Wide Effort

At Keller Williams Realty, they have a charity arm of the company, a 501(3)(c) called KW Cares. "We're teaching our people the higher purpose of business and the joy of giving, sharing and caring," says Mo Anderson. The idea for the group came about when Mo was the CEO of Keller Williams. It was something being done in Austin, Texas, and they came to Mo and asked if they could take it national.

"It's just amazing, when Katrina hit I simply got on the phone with our wonderful people and I said to them I need five million dollars. I need it by December thirty-first at midnight." They had fifty thousand agents at the time, so Mo told them she needed the equivalent of a hundred dollar donation per agent. They didn't make a donation mandatory, but they wanted to share with their agents in need. "Seven hundred and sixty eight agents were affected. About three hundred fifty of them lost everything they had in Katrina, and I want you to know that $5.3 million came in between the end of August and December thirty-first.

HEAT Moment

Mo Anderson continues to Honor the lives of those afflicted by tragedy through the compassionate contributions of KW Cares.

Next the company implemented the Heart to Heart program, where market centers would adopt families. "I have seen market centers get car dealerships to donate a car and they would drive it to New Orleans and give it to that family who needed it. I have seen the most amazing things in the whole wide world." After Katrina, they helped people affected by the tornado in Joplin, Missouri in 2011.

They also started Red Day, which is where each year, on Mo's birthday, everyone stops selling real estate for the day and does something to give back to the community. "The things they have done are just incredible! All over North America there were projects going on that would just blow your mind. From renovating a special needs facility to mowing lawns for the elderly to building a house for Habitat for Humanity. I could go on and on." Mo says she wants the company to be known as the company that cares not just about their own people, but about the community.

Protecting the Environment

George McKerrow and his partner, Ted Turner, are giving back to the environment in a rather unique way. They are helping to reestablish the bison population. "We've succeeded in bringing bison to America's table. We've created a market and we've protected one of North America's greatest assets, the buffalo. Bison are native to North America. They were an endangered species." This is a great example of entrepreneurship filling a niche and simultaneously protecting a natural resource.

"When we started Ted's Montana Grill there was almost half the number of bison that there are alive in the world today. We created a marketplace for them to ensure their survival. That may sound odd to some people, but without bison being a commodity they're an endangered species." They have also helped bison ranchers who were struggling entrepreneurs. There you go. You just received an extremely practical lesson in economics—specifically, the law of supply and demand in a free market society!

Hot Seat

✓ What are some ways that you as an individual, or your company, will be able to give back? Will it be in monetary or product donations, service, or volunteer work?

STAND IN THE HEAT
Chapter Twenty

A New Paradigm for Entrepreneurship

"Coming together is a beginning; keeping together is progress; working together is success."

- Henry Ford

The most successful entrepreneurs tend to be mavericks – nonconformists who follow no leader, fiercely independent creative thinkers who follow no herd, self-made men and women who follow no one else's "formula for success." Yet, no one does it alone. No one. Virtually every entrepreneur I've known or studied credits his or her success largely to the people on their team and in their inner circle. The greatest entrepreneurs of our time deliberately and continually build mutually beneficial relationships with a wide network of collaborators, mentors, advisers, innovators, thought leaders, and supporters.

Few new and aspiring entrepreneurs realize that. Fewer still take advantage of the peer expertise and people power available to them, much less seek out the human connections that are so critical to one's survival, sanity, and success in the uniquely challenging world of entrepreneurship. Instead, many of us just go it alone – naively, stubbornly, and far too often, unsuccessfully embarking upon the long, hard journey of solo entrepreneurship.

Fortunately for me, several years ago I met a remarkable person who helped change my mindset and approach to entrepreneurship. I've had the privilege of interviewing many incredible entrepreneurs from all walks of life, from all across the United States. There are entrepreneurs, and then there is the "entrepreneur's entrepreneur," Mitchell Schlimer.

Mitch has been a serial and social entrepreneur for more than thirty-five years. In addition to being an inventor and accomplished photographer, Mitch has founded six businesses, including Mitch Schlimer Tennis Centers, a video production business, and an advertising agency called Impac International. He is also a co-founder and board member of the Magic Wand Foundation, an amazing organization dedicated to empowering youth around the world and sharing "the 7 mindsets to live your ultimate life." In dissecting ten years' worth of interviews with entrepreneurs and successful people on Mitch's *Let's Talk Business Radio* program and through studying the most successful people in the world throughout history, Mitch and his fellow Magic Wand Foundation co-founders – Scott Shickler, Jeff Waller, and Juan Casimiro – determined that one's mindsets, not just one's skill sets, are critical to one's success.

In 1993, with a vision to create the "ESPN for entrepreneurs," Mitch founded Let's Talk Business Network (LTBN), which provides consulting, coaching, educational, and other support services to entrepreneurs, business owners, CEOs, and youth. As the creator and host of the national *Let's Talk Business Radio*, Mitch has interviewed more than 750 (and counting) successful entrepreneurs and authors, including such notables as Sir Richard Branson, Wally Amos, Anita Roddick, Fred DeLuca, Jim Collins, and one of my heroes, Jack Canfield.

Mitch's passion for the advancement and expansion of entrepreneurship around the globe led him to found the original Entrepreneurship Hall of Fame (EHOF) in 2002. In late 2011 he founded the EpiCenter – the global center for entrepreneurship, philanthropy, and innovation as well as the home of EHOF. Mitch serves as Executive Director of both the EpiCenter and the Entrepreneurship Hall of Fame.

Mitch Schlimer is truly at the epicenter of entrepreneurship, and you won't find a more passionate and dedicated advocate for entrepreneurs. Who better to share these concluding insights on withstanding the heat of entrepreneurship and forging your own entrepreneurial success?

Your Simple Idea Could Be the Next Big Thing

One of Mitch's most successful ideas came to him when he was a tennis pro, coaching players of all levels of ability. "Every time I'd try to explain top spin or under spin to beginning or average players, they'd look at me like a deer caught in headlights," he says. "Eventually, I realized they didn't understand because they literally could not see the ball spin."

At the time, tennis balls were a single color, either white or yellow? Mitch noticed that when you threw a two-colored Nerf ball, you could see the spin. "I thought, if a Nerf ball can have two different colors, why can't a tennis ball?"

Soon after, Mitch and his intellectual property attorney, Irwin Telcher, filed a patent for a two-tone (yellow-and-orange) tennis ball. "It was a very simple idea, born solely out of my desire to help people see and understand the spin of a tennis ball. But lo and behold, it became much bigger than I could have imagined. That ball is still being sold, more than thirty years later."

When Mitch's yellow-and-orange tennis ball first hit the market, a lot of people probably smacked their foreheads and said, "Why didn't I think of that?" The answer to that rhetorical question is that innovators like Mitch think outside the box to create unique solutions to common problems. Sometimes, the best solution is a simple idea. But it takes a bit of creative genius to come up with a simple idea that's marketable, and it takes a lot of chutzpah to then bring that idea to market.

Recognize and Seize Unique Opportunities

For several years early in his career, Mitch was the head pro and founding owner of Mitch Schlimer Tennis Centers in Houston, Texas. He had two tennis clubs, each with eight courts and a pro shop. After being robbed a few times and receiving inadequate compensation on his insurance claims, Mitch was frustrated. "The insurance company always said the same thing: 'We need receipts and photos of all the stolen merchandise.' You can imagine how many photos we'd need to maintain a visual record of the entire inventory in the pro shops," he says.

Thanks to his background in communications, Mitch realized that video was the perfect medium for documenting and providing proof of inventory for a business or belongings in a home in the event of a robbery, flood, fire, or other loss. So he sold his tennis centers and founded Diversified Video Services. "As they say, necessity is the mother of invention."

Before long, Mitch not only was videotaping inventory for businesses and possessions for homeowners and renters, he also was doing video yearbooks, wedding videos, deposition videos, video wills, and sales videos. Soon, he began franchising the business at a local level.

"These days, everybody has a video recorder. But at the time, camcorders and VCRs were cutting-edge technologies, and nobody was offering video-recording services to businesses and consumers."

Mitch recognized a new opportunity in the marketplace and went for it – one of the hallmarks of successful entrepreneurs.

Create a Business You Can Exit, Not a Job You're Dependent On

Having started and owned several businesses and having coached, interviewed, mentored, and worked with thousands of entrepreneurs, Mitch knows firsthand how difficult it is to build a successful, profitable company. Even more difficult, he says, is building a business you can sell.

"Less than one percent of entrepreneurs build a business they can exit," he says. "What that tells you is that 99 percent create a job for themselves, which at best provides a living, rather than create a business they can sell at a profit."

Just as successful parents teach and prepare their children to one day live without them, so, too, do successful entrepreneurs plan and prepare for their businesses to go on without them. A truly successful business is one in which the founder can sell their business and go on to do the next thing they're passionate about. Mitch has been fortunate to do that twice.

Build a Network of Champions

"The best thing about being an entrepreneur is the freedom to be yourself, do your own thing, and pursue something that matters to you," Mitch says. "The worst thing is the high level of ambiguity and instability."

Mitch's strong desire to help entrepreneurs, innovators, and business leaders maximize their potential and achieve success is why he created Let's Talk Business Network in 1993, the Entrepreneurship Hall of Fame in 2002, and the EpiCenter in late 2011. This vision emerged in the early 1990s, when Mitch, then in his mid-thirties, started doing some soul-searching: *Why am I here? What is life all about? What do I know best? What has the journey of being an entrepreneur taught me?*

"My first thought was how isolating and lonely entrepreneurship can be. Second was how many things are totally out of your control. Third was the unacceptably high rate of start-up failures in this country." Based on those realizations, Mitch decided there needed to be a place where entrepreneurs could come to brainstorm, empower, support, and learn from one another.

"Great entrepreneurs are voracious, lifelong learners." They also are network-builders who understand the importance of creating and nurturing strong relationships. "Turning an idea into something tangible takes a lot of great people who believe in the idea and the leader. Ideas are cheap; a good team is invaluable."

I also suggest finding mentors, joining peer groups, and putting together an advisory board, whose expertise and encouragement will help guide and empower you on the journey of entrepreneurship.

Make It about More than You

"I like to help people in any way I can. That is what drives me." Mitch's two-tone tennis ball was a simple way to help others; his Let's Talk Business Network, Entrepreneurship Hall of Fame, and EpiCenter are big ideas designed to help the millions of people who are, or who dream of, starting and running and growing a successful business.

But helping others is more than merely something Mitch likes to do. It goes beyond wanting to feel good about his life and his work. It is a brilliant business strategy that has proven to be integral not only to Mitch's success but also to the success of countless other outstanding entrepreneurs.

In Mitch's considerable experience and observation, "doing something that truly matters, that goes far and above building a successful business and making a buck," is the single most important component of entrepreneurial success and being a true social entrepreneur. It is what empowers and enables you to stand in the heat, stay cool under pressure, and turn your dream into a reality.

"Don't make it about you. I know for a fact that people who do make it all about themselves eventually see the good people on their team leave because they feel like just a pawn in someone else's game.

"Have a vision and a mission that's bigger than you. Do something that makes a positive difference in the world. Create something you believe in and that other people can believe in, benefit from, and get behind. Build something you can leave behind. "When you do that, you dramatically increase your odds of success." In fact, Mitch suggests creating a business whose primary mission is to contribute something of significant value to the world.

Today, entrepreneurs who create businesses or organizations or institutions specifically designed to do good in the world are called "social entrepreneurs." Mitch Schlimer has been a social entrepreneur for over thirty years, long before the term was coined or the idea even conceived.

A true visionary in the world of entrepreneurship, Mitch is focused on his largest social venture yet – building the EpiCenter, the home of the Entrepreneurship Hall of Fame.

Time for You to Take Action

<u>Start Doing Now</u>

✓ Model Success
  ❖ Identify a person who has done exactly what you want to do and copy them.

✓ Put your goals in writing
  ❖ Have clearly written goals and read them morning and night with emotion.

✓ Continually expand your comfort zone
  ❖ All growth takes place outside of our comfort zone.

✓ Create a strategy for dealing with stress
  ❖ Entrepreneurship can be stressful. Be prepared in advance to deal with stress.

✓ Accept full responsibility for everything in your life
  ❖ Taking full responsibility for every aspect of our lives creates the space for growth.

✓ Read a book on the subject of your interest
  ❖ No matter what you want to accomplish there is an authority on the subject.

✓ Make a "Grateful For" list
  ❖ The quickest way to increase your income is to remain grateful for what you already have.

✓ Take action in your fleeting moments of inspiration
  ❖ Do something in those inspired moment as the window of opportunity can be very narrow.

✓ Do something every day that moves you closer to your dream
   ❖ Consistency is key. Remember, the turtle beat the hare!

✓ Reframe the word "failure"
   ❖ Really, there is no such thing as "failure"; only outcome. Become aware of how you label your experiences.

<u>Start Doing in the Next 3 Months</u>

✓ Write down your Top 100 goals
   ❖ This can be a challenging exercise. Once you get past the selfish, material objects, you will start to get in touch with your true purpose.

✓ Create a Vision Board
   ❖ Having a crystal clear vision of where you want to go is critical. Let your imagination run wild!

✓ Put affirmations on your bathroom mirror
   ❖ Read your affirmations with passion and as Dr. Wayne Dyer says, "Assume the feeling of your wish fulfilled."

✓ Keep a written list of your top three 90 day goals in your pocket
   ❖ Your most important short-term goals need "top of mind" presence.

✓ Find an accountability partner
   ❖ Most of us avoid accountability, but all of us need accountability.

✓ Join a support group
  ❖ As Dr. Kathleen Hall advises, become part of a supportive tribe.

✓ BE the person you dream of becoming
  ❖ Act as if you have already become the person you want to be and treat others as if they have already become the people you want them to be.

✓ Confront your fear
  ❖ Run toward the fire and address your fear. Courage is the act of taking action in spite of your fear.

Start Doing in the Next 6 Months

✓ Go public with a big, hairy, audacious goal on Facebook
  ❖ Have the guts to announce to the world who you are and what you intend to accomplish!

✓ Write a mission/vision statement

✓ Write an executive summary/business plan

✓ Make a "Chicken List" (people you are afraid to call) and contact them
  ❖ It has never ceased to amaze me what you can get in life if you only ask with confidence. Be BOLD!

✓ Create your personal Board of Advisors
  ❖ Surround yourself with people who have strengths that offset your weaknesses. Include people who will call you out on your shortcomings.

✓ Find a Mentor
The right mentor can massively shorten your runway to success.

✓ Constantly expand your network
As Harvey Mackay says, "Dig your well before you are thirsty!"

Start Doing in the Next 12 Months

✓ Mentor someone else
❖ Pay it forward. Reach down and lend someone else a helping hand.

✓ Teach a class on it
If you want to learn something, teach a class on it. Be willing to put yourself in the hot seat and be vulnerable. Doing is the ultimate form of learning.

✓ Serve your community

✓ Clean up your credit report
A strong FICO score can will allow you borrow funds to expand your business.

✓ Take night classes on business
Invest in yourself. It's never too late to start over.

✓ Develop a relationship with a personal banker
Find a banker who believes in you and your story.

✓ Start giving money away before you have a lot of money
This act can be difficult when we are "paycheck to paycheck," but it creates an abundance mentality. Money is literally everywhere!

Suggested Reading List

Non-Fiction

177 Mental Toughness Secrets of the World Class – Steve Siebold

All You Can Do is All You Can Do – A.L. Williams

Awaken the Giant Within – Anthony Robbins

Between a Rock and Hard Place – Aron Ralston

Built from Scratch – Arthur Blank and Bernie Marcus

Glenn Beck's Common Sense – Glenn Beck

Goals! How to Get Everything You Want — Faster Than You Ever Thought Possible – Brian Tracy

Good to Great – Jim Collins

How to Win Friends & Influence People – Dale Carnegie

Lead the Field – Earl Nightingale

Leadership Secrets of Attila the Hun – Wess Roberts, Ph.D.

Lincoln on Leadership – Donald T. Phillips

Psycho-Cybernetics – Maxwell Maltz, M.D.

Rich Dad Poor Dad – Robert T. Kiyosaki

Rich Dad's Cashflow Quadrant – Robert T. Kiyosaki

Sam Walton: Made in America – Sam Walton

Secrets of Power Persuasion – Roger Dawson

Seeds of Greatness –Denis Waitley

See You at the Top – Zig Ziglar

Success Through A Positive Mental Attitude – Napoleon Hill

Swim with the Sharks Without Being Eaten Alive – Harvey B. Mackay

The 7 Habits of Highly Effective People – Stephen R. Covey

The Closers – Ben Gay III

The Compound Effect – Darren Hardy

The E Myth – Michael E. Gerber

The Energy Bus – Jon Gordon

The Magic of Thinking Big – David J. Schwartz, Ph.D.

The Millionaire Real Estate Agent – Gary Keller

The One-Minute Manager – Ken Blanchard and Spencer Johnson

The Power of Intention – Dr. Wayne W. Dyer

The Power of Positive Thinking – Norman Vincent Peale
The Psychology of Selling – Brian Tracy
The Seven Spiritual Laws of Success – Deepak Chopra
The West Point Way of Leadership – Col. Larry R. Donnithorne (Ret.)
Think and Grow Rich – Napoleon Hill
Trump: The Art of the Deal – Donald Trump with Tony Schwartz
Unlimited Power – Anthony Robbins
Where Have All the Leaders Gone? – Lee Iaccoca
You Can't Teach a Kid to Ride a Bike at a Seminar – David H. Sandler
You'll See It When You Believe It – Dr. Wayne W. Dyer*

Fiction
Atlas Shrugged – Ayn Rand

*The first book I read twice

References

"About Joyce." MillionaireMoms.com.
   http://www.millionairemom.com/node/113.

"About Ted's Montana Grill: George McKerrow, Jr." Ted's Montana
   Grill, Inc. http://www.tedsmontanagrill.com/george.html.

Beck, Glenn. *Glenn Beck's Common Sense – The Case Against an Out-of-
   Control Government, Inspired by Thomas Paine.* Threshold Editions,
   2009.

"Brad's Story."
   http://www.bradsugars.com/page.php?page=bradsstory.

Brain, Marshall. "How Laughter Works." How Stuff Works Online.

   http://science.howstuffworks.com/environmental/life/human-
   biology/laughter4.htm.

BrainyQuote. http://www.brainyquote.com/.

"Dave Liniger." RE/MAX Corporate Information.
   http://www.remax.com/nationalcorp/biographies/dave_liniger.a
   spx

"Dr. Kathleen Hall." http://www.drkathleenhall.com/.

"Entrepreneur." *Merriam-Webster Unabridged Collegiate Dictionary.*
   http://unabridged.merriam-webster.com/.

"Executive Biographies - Mo Anderson." Keller Williams Realty.
   http://www.kw.com/kw/execbios.html.

"Firemen Build a Franchise." *How I Made My Millions.* CNBC.

"Get to Know Us." Keller Williams Realty, Inc.
   http://www.kw.com/kw/aboutus.html.

Harkins, Phil and Keith Hollihan. *Everybody Wins: The Story and Lessons
   Behind RE/MAX.*   Wiley, 2006.

"Heather's Story." Yummie By Heather Thompson.
   http://www.yummielife.com/heather-thomson.html.

"Hermain Cain. Facebook.
   https://www.facebook.com/THEHermanCain?sk=info

"Herman Cain Returns to News/Talk WSB." January 18, 2012. WSBRadio.com. http://www.wsbradio.com/news/online/herman-cain-returns-newstalk-wsb/nGP5m/.

"I. Pano Karatassos." Ellis Island Medal of Honor. http://neco.org/awards/recipients/ipkaratassos.html.

"Lisa Levison." LinkedIn. http://www.linkedin.com/pub/lisa-levison/15/7ba/a3a.

"Meet Trish McCarty." http://www.trishmccarty.com/.

"Our Story." Decontamination Restoration Services. http://drskits.com/.

"Pano I. Karatassos." Buckhead Life Restaurant Group. http://www.buckheadrestaurants.com/kyma/chef/.

"RE/MAX Corporate Information." RE/MAX, LLC. http://www.remax.com/national-corp/index.aspx.

Robbins, Anthony. *Unlimited Power.* Simon & Schuster, 2001.

"Scott Goodknight." LinkedIn. http://www.linkedin.com/pub/scottgoodknight/19/938/176.

"Stroock Client Yummie Tummie Settles Patent Infringement and Invalidity Lawsuits with Maidenform." Stroock. http://www.stroock.com/sitecontent.cfm?contentID=53&itemID=347.

"Trish McCarty." LinkedIn. http://www.linkedin.com/in/trishmccarty.

"Wendy Reed, Executive Vice President Strategic Alliances." The TAS Group Leadership Team. http://www.thetasgroup.com/bio-wendy-reed.php.

About the Author

Glenn Carver is a native of Atlanta, Georgia, where he currently resides with his wife, Lisa, and son, Grant. He is a speaker, author, statewide television host, entrepreneur, Proud Papa, and student of life. He has flown an airplane solo, been skydiving, bungee jumping, rappelling, attended Jim Russell Racers Driving School, and done stand-up comedy at the Punchline in Atlanta. He loves his family, beautiful music, speedy cars, engaging people, and laughing until it hurts!

Glenn has a passion for free enterprise, capitalism, and entrepreneurship. With a total commitment to personal development and human potential, he has demonstrated through his sincere communication style how to motivate and inspire business professionals throughout North America and South Africa. He is a world-class communicator who is able to connect and develop rapport with audiences of any nature. He has an in-depth understanding of human nature, business process, and the psychology of selling.

Glenn studied Real Estate and Finance (when he wasn't socializing) at the University of Georgia from 1985 to 1989. In 2004, he pulled the trigger on his dream of entering the field of public speaking. He launched his speaking career in Los Angeles by promoting a sales training seminar called "Selling Outside of the Box" created by Paul Schween. A year later, Glenn went to work for Richard Robbins International based in Toronto. RRI is an achievement coaching organization focused in the real estate industry. From 2008 to 2009, Glenn worked for Sales Partners which is an international, business coaching organization founded by Blair Singer. Blair Singer is a "Rich Dad Advisor" to Robert Kiyosaki, author of the international best seller, *Rich Dad Poor Dad*.

Glenn Carver is the Chief Entrepreneurial Officer of HEAT Ventures, LLC, a media production company designed to inspire people worldwide to realize their greatest potential through his speaking, writing, television production, and online information products.

He is on the Advisory Board of the EpiCenter which is the home of the Entrepreneurship Hall of Fame in Atlanta, Ga.

In February 2010, Glenn was inspired to write his first book on entrepreneurship called Stand in the Heat: Lessons from Legendary Entrepreneurs on Staying Cool under Pressure. Stand in the HEAT is a survival guide for entrepreneurs and it is Glenn's personal mission to empower today's entrepreneurs with inspiration and strategies for long-term success.

Stand in the HEAT received early praise from personal development legend Brian Tracy, who said, "This could be one of the most important books ever written." In September 2012, Glenn was interviewed by Inc. magazine on how corporations can cultivate the "entrepreneurial spirit" within their culture.